VISIONS *from* HEAVEN

Wendy Alec

WOUNDED WARRIORS
OUT OF THE WILDERNESS

WARBOYS PUBLISHING

Published by Warboys Publishing (Ireland) Limited
77, Sir John Rogerson's Quay, Dublin 2, Ireland

Unless otherwise stated, Scripture quotations are from the Amplified Bible. Copyright © 1954, 1958, 1962, 1964, 1965, 1987 by the Lockman Foundation.

Scripture quotations marked NIV are from the Holy Bible, New International Version®, NIV®. Copyright © 1973, 1978, 1984, 2011 by Biblica, Inc.® Used by permission. All rights reserved worldwide.

Scripture quotations marked KJV are from the King James Version and reproduced by permission of Cambridge University Press, the Crown's patentee in the UK.

Scripture quotations marked NKJV are from the New King James Version®. Copyright © 1982 by Thomas Nelson. Used by permission. All rights reserved.

ISBN: 978–0–9928063–4–7 (paperback)
ISBN: 978–0–9928063–3–0 (Kindle)

Cover design by W. Alec, C. Bown and Studiogearbox
Typesetting and eBook by CRB Associates, Potterhanworth, Lincolnshire, UK
Printed in the USA

ARE YOU STRUGGLING WITH LOSS, HOPE DEFERRED, DIVORCE, ABANDONMENT?

Jesus said,

"THE SPIRIT OF THE LORD IS UPON ME, BECAUSE HE HATH ANOINTED ME TO PREACH THE GOSPEL TO THE POOR; HE HATH SENT ME TO HEAL THE BROKEN HEARTED . . . TO PREACH DELIVERANCE TO THE CAPTIVES AND RECOVERING OF SIGHT TO THE BLIND, TO SET AT LIBERTY THEM THAT ARE BRUISED . . . TO PREACH THE ACCEPTABLE YEAR OF THE LORD."

(Luke 4:18–19 KJV)

NOTE FROM THE PUBLISHER

This material is taken from, and was previously published on, Wendy Alec's public Facebook page. Following many requests from followers we have assembled all the posts into this one volume along with additional content.

CONTENTS

Dedication   7

Daddy, I Can't Dance   9

Prayer Dedication   10

My Secret Place with the Father – Opening Prayer   11

Introduction   13

Tel-Aviv, Israel June 1, 2014   18

Seer Journey Begins   21

Conversation with the Father, Ministry Face-Off   24

You Called Me Out of Darkness   30

The Wounded Warrior Lost in the Woods   35

Jesus and the Royal Guard   37

Prophetic Seer Interpretation of Wounded Warriors
    in the Woods   41

The Battleground   46

The Lion Roars   50

Prophetic Word – Don't Lie Down on the Battlefield   52

The Torture Chamber   57

You Are Beautiful   62

The Yellow Brick Road – Hope Deferred No More.   66

The Baggage   69

Courage – a New Season   71

The Season of Transition   75

Shifting from Transition   76

When It's Only I Who See . . .   79

In the Night Season   81

The Rose   84

Beloved Warriors   86

You Are An Overcomer   90

"The Sound of My Army Has Been Heard
    in the Kingdom of Darkness"   92

You Were Born for Such a Day   94

New Life – War and Worship   97

You Are a Dreamer   99

Season of Loneliness   102

The Father's Love   104

The Fairy Tale   105

The Birthday Party Dress   107

A Walk with Jesus in His Garden   110

The Jigsaw Puzzle   115

Satan's Trophy Room   118

The Last Push – Flying by Instruments   123

Joseph   127

Seer Encounter from the Father   131

Your Gentleness   134

The Airlift   137

Lazarus Is Dead   139

Stretched to the Limit   142

My First Year – a Little Bit of My Story   145

Epilogue Wounded Warriors   151

Final Thoughts and Prayers   163

Contact Details   167

DEDICATION

This book is dedicated to the most courageous warrior and prophet I have ever known.

I had the greatest privilege and honor to know him as my beloved friend, Kim Clement.

Kim, I love you.

We will never forget you.

Your legacy transcends all we know as space and time and continues through eternity.

How we will miss you here on Earth, but your incredible assignment continues . . . as you walk hand in hand with the Father in His garden. Love forever,

Wendy x

This book is also dedicated to the most amazing tribe of warriors on my public Facebook page and especially to our incredible Royal Guard intercessors and all in the U.K. and U.S. who have laid their lives down in prayer for myself and the media mantle I carry . . . I love you with a fervent love, beloved warriors . . . the best is yet to come.

DADDY, I CAN'T DANCE

To all those who have lost heart while contending in the fierce heat of the battle and who feel too weary and hopeless to dance.

Maybe you can't dance because your heart has been broken and betrayed.

Maybe you feel you can't dance because through the years so many dreams have been deferred and today you find yourself heartsick.

Maybe you have been temporarily derailed because of infirmity or chronic illness.

Maybe you have experienced a devastating loss of a loved one.

And your tutu is hanging in a closet and your ballet shoes are dusty from disuse.

But today, your incredible Father, your ultimate Daddy, is standing in His garden, His arms outstretched to you.

His smile never wavering.

And He whispers,

"Beloved daughter/son of my heart,

Come, come, run into my arms."

So, put your dancing shoes on,

Whether they are ballet shoes

Or sparkling-red Dorothy "Wizard of Oz" shoes,

Or Steve Madden boots . . .

For, beloved . . .

Today, the most beautiful Emperor,

The Father from whom all fatherhood is named,

The Father of all compassion . . . is wooing you back into the dance.

PRAYER DEDICATION

*T*hese pages are written for all those who are broken hearted . . .
To those who feel trapped in the icy grip of pain, abandonment and trauma . . .

And to those whose hearts and emotions have been so bruised in this last season . . .

Oh, how Jesus loves you . . .

And where maybe some aspects of the Church have placed emphasis on other issues . . .

And many broken hearts have been relegated to feeling under a veil of shame . . .

Your heart healing ranks so high on Heaven's agenda that Jesus declared that is why he came . . .

O Father, I pray that the anointing of Jesus himself, our mighty King of kings, will pour from these pages to bind up the broken hearted . . . set the captives free . . . and heal each one who is bruised . . .

O Lord Jesus . . . let your great compassion flow and heal, bind up and restore hope in these pages . . .

Jesus, you are our balm of Gilead.

Bind up our wounds as only you can.

Deliver us from every hope deferred and trauma trapped in our souls.

Set every secret captive place in our hearts free . . .

For thine is the kingdom,

The power,

And the glory

Forever and ever

Amen.

MY SECRET PLACE WITH THE
FATHER – OPENING PRAYER

*B*eloved, beloved of God, as you start to read these pages, I pray and release, in the mighty and tender name of Jesus, fresh hope from Heaven itself.

Father, I release encounter and your presence and your manifest glory right now into this precious heart.

Father, we ask for a release of angelic visitation, the eternal comfort and counsel of the beloved Holy Spirit and magnificent encounters with the tender, overwhelming mercies and compassion of the love of the Father.

Amen

INTRODUCTION

Beloved friend,

In my own walk and history with the Father, I always believed that when we went through fiery trials and trauma, it would naturally draw us closer to our Lord Jesus and the Father.

But, I was wrong.

In my own experience of pain and talking to many other ministers and sons and daughters going through a fiery, seemingly deserted place, I have discovered that it becomes much, much harder than any of us may care to admit to connect with Heaven in our times of utter despair.

Our beloved Holy Spirit reminded me that even our beloved Lord Jesus, when fighting for his soul's survival in Gethsemane, sweated drops of blood.

And on the cross at the point of his greatest anguish, he cried out, "Father, Father, why have you forsaken me?"

But how Jesus understands . . . Oh, how near he is to your breaking heart.

How he understands your infinite humanity.

How he draws near to your silent scream, caressing your head on your tear-stained pillow, whispering to you.

"I am with you always.

"You are not forsaken,

"This pain will pass."

Truly, truly he IS the Lover of our souls.

These pages are written for all those who have been facing a barren wilderness of transition, living day to day in what has seemed to be an eternal winter.

To those that when you have woken every morning, you have felt you have been clinging on by just a thread, hoping desperately that today would be the day that the dormant bulbs would break through the ground, that the bare branches of your life would bud into the blossoms of springtime.

And some of you have literally cried out:

Father . . . Jesus . . . What is happening?

Miracles used to pour upon my life so easily,

Your goodness in the land of the living used to shower all around me.

DISCERN THE TIMES AND THE SEASONS

And the Father said this:

"Wendy . . . tell my beloved children that when they are under the greatest, seemingly unrelenting attack, to still their hearts and discern the seasons and the times."

The Father spoke, and His heart was so filled with compassion, but He also spoke with a divine urgency. He said, "There has been a violent shift of strategy in the warfare from the demonic powers and principalities in this season.

"The enemy of your souls well knows that his time is running down and in this past five-year season, he has launched all-out warfare against my beloved champions.

"My courageous ones have clung to me with every fiber of their beings, but as the season of wilderness continued and to so many of my beloved it seemed that the heavens were brass, many of my called-out ones started to lose their grip on my promises to them, their hearts became heavy with deferred hope and many in this past season of transition began to feel forsaken.

"For it has been a season where many . . . so many have in the natural been violently assailed and have lost so much.

"Some have lost businesses.

"Others have lost ministries.

"Many have been struggling with infirmity.

"Homes, families, husbands and wives have been lost.

"Children have been lost.

"Oh, how I have heard the desperate weeping of mothers who have lost their sons and daughters,

"For my heart has broken as their heart has broken . . .

"And so many of my champions became perplexed and bewildered crying out to me,

"'Father, where . . . oh, where is your saving hand?'

"For there has been a great and ferocious battle in the Heavenlies in this past season;

"And even as the Archangel Michael was sent to Gabriel and my greatly beloved Daniel and it took him 21 days to break through to victory,

"So satanic princes and powers and principalities have marshalled themselves in this past season, these past five years . . .

"To obstruct and delay and defer my beloved called-out ones' promises."

Then I heard the Father say,

"My beloved child, Satan's primary objective was to target my champions' hearts, those who have loved me with all of their being, those who have laid their lives down in serving me.

"That they would be tempted beyond their endurance and cry . . .

"'Father . . . you have forsaken me . . . you have deserted me' . . . as the enemy of your soul endeavored to imprint his own nature upon my faithfulness, my goodness, my great mercies and compassion.

"Your enemy is the father of lies.

"He is the destroyer of dreams.

"There is no truth to be found in him.

"And this day I declare to you, that as you have stood in the furnace and in the barren wilderness . . . the portals of Heaven's favor are opening above you . . .

"A new season is descending from Heaven over my sons . . . over my daughters . . .

"A season of breakthrough.

"A season of unprecedented favor.

"A season of restoration.

"And restitution.

"A season where my infinite goodness and mercies are about to cascade upon your life with fresh rain.

"With an oasis in the wilderness,

"Where the barren desert will bloom,

"Where the mirages of the burning desert season will be mirages no more,

But tangible dreams fulfilled."

And so the Father would whisper to your heart this day,

"Child of courage,

"You have so moved my heart;

"It is a new day

"One more step, O valiant one,

"For when you were stumbling and you lost all hope

"I was there

"Loving you,

"Carrying you.

"Look back in wonder

"And you will see that it is MY footprints in the sand."

Beloved hearts, I pray that as you read these pages, and as you spend time in your own sacred and secret place with Jesus, the Father and beloved Holy Spirit, that not only will you receive the comfort of the Father, but that assignments of the enemy on your mind, will, emotions and circumstances will start to literally break off your life.

That there will be an impartation of beauty for ashes.

Hope for despair.

Joy for mourning.

And refreshing, strength, laughter and joy for the dreams still ahead for you as you prepare to enter the most exciting season of your life.

The Father has kept you for such a time as this.

He has been there at every turn and twist in your road.

He has carried you in His arms when you were too weary to even place one foot before the other.

And now, oh, so beloved of His heart . . .

He is wooing you back,

For it is your time to dance . . .

Love forever,

From my heart to yours,

Wendy

TEL-AVIV, ISRAEL
June 1, 2014

"*Y*our divorce is finalized."

I received the telephone call confirming the end of twenty-seven years of a marriage that had not only produced two amazing children, but that had also birthed one of the biggest global religious networks in the world – GOD TV.

It was the end of both a personal and ministry era.

I would so love to write and tell you that my healing was instantaneous. That my heart was rapidly healed. That this was a quick and painless, practical and legal process. But, as I have since learned from thousands of others of the most incredible warriors from all around the world, most of us were left bleeding out on the battlefield, scrabbling for a way to survive the pain in our hearts that never seemed to leave.

Not sleeping, yet somehow waking to another dreaded No-Man's Land when daylight hit. In our pajamas with our faithful cats (and dogs, though I lost my two adored Ridgebacks in the cause), trying to martial enough strength to keep the little that was left of our lives and sanity together. And for many of us, to earn enough to take care of our abandoned families.

Waking up in the early hours of the morning, thoughts reeling. I'm getting older, how will I provide for myself? I've worked so hard all my life and basically have nothing material to show for it.

I wandered around like the Israelites in the wilderness for three years, spending over a year in Israel, then Norway and finally back to the U.K. trying to put the shattered pieces of my life back together.

Fighting a fierce legal battle for my book and TV rights and my publishing company which held all my intellectual property. Losing all the money invested in our family home – a story too long to describe here. And, finally, knowing that it was time to move on from GOD TV, the ministry we had sacrificed almost everything for to concentrate on my mandate – creative evangelism – but missing my GOD TV family desperately.

I don't share this as a victim, but because I have discovered that there are so many thousands of men and women experiencing exactly the same brutal circumstances, and that, beloved one, as you read these pages, you don't think, well it's all right for Wendy, she must have been totally protected. Beautiful heart, my entire life was ravaged, just like so many of you. I've been there. I've walked the harrowing walk.

Bill Johnson once said something to me that rang so deep in my spirit and I have never forgotten his words: "Wendy, so often people miss their miracles being in the process because they are looking for their miracle and don't realize that more often than not their miracle is in the process."

This book is dedicated to all who have lost husbands and wives who they thought would be their protectors in their old age. To all who have lost homes, jobs, income, treasured pets, furniture . . .

But most of all, to all you, oh, so courageous wounded warriors, so adored by the Father, who are still lying or sitting in the battlefield, bewildered, vulnerable, bleeding from intense wounds of the heart, crying out to Jesus for hope.

I pray that these seer encounters from Heaven (many from when I was facing such agonizing pain and trauma) will minister to you from the Father Himself. And, as He takes you by the hand and walks with you, and at times carries you so tenderly through His garden in Heaven . . . holding your weary hands and kissing your head as He whispers to you. "This is only a transition, precious one. Hold on. Hold on, with all your courage, hold on."

So here, beloved warrior family, whom I so admire and respect for your courage, your perseverance, your love for your brothers and sisters in Christ and who only through sheer incredible 'guts' are still standing.

Truly to you, the VICTOR'S CROWN is yours!

From my heart, we have been forged together in the fire of affliction and the greater love that has been forged between us is incredible.

Let our journey begin. Onward and upward on our yellow brick road to the Father's throne room, where all things are restored, all loss is regained, all heartaches are soothed and bound up by the lover of our souls and where brand-new rainbows of fulfilment and earthly dreams await us. The goodness of God in the land of the living. Thank you for your incredible love for me; it has forged an indescribable love for you. Let us together take the first step of Heaven's journey. This is for you.

SEER JOURNEY BEGINS

DINNER WITH BENNY HINN

I remember having dinner with Benny Hinn after the most incredible, anointed service that GOD TV had hosted in the U.K. My life and our little family at that point were completely intact and I had absolutely no conception of the tsunami that was on its way. Pastor Benny was sharing about his and Susanne's divorce, the sheer impact of it and how he had experienced some of the very darkest moments of his life.

But tonight he and his lovely ex-wife, Susanne, were now reconciled and restored and had such a heart for marriage restoration.

But the truth is I simply couldn't relate.

Divorce was a word that was completely cerebral to me. It was totally alien to my world and, although I felt badly for those who were divorced, I never gave it more than a moment's thought.

That was then.

Over three years later and having lived through the absolute devastation of my marriage, with my family and ministry having been brutally ripped apart emotionally, I can never, never be complacent about it again.

And my heart and intense compassion and utter admiration goes out to many, many in the Church at this time, those who have been the targets of this attack by the enemy. The devastation is indescribable.

LOSS

The tsunami hits.

Your best friend and companion through years of marriage is gone forever.

The sheer, agonizing loneliness.

Sleeping alone in a king-size bed.

No one to dream with.

Laugh with.

Cry with.

Plan the future with. Just silence.

Night after night.

Waking up to another surreal day of attempting to exist in a world that literally has been blown to smithereens.

So many of us lost our homes, our income, furniture and beloved pets, left to live like nomads scrabbling desperately for some far-flung escape route out of the nightmare back into survival.

Make no mistake . . . I did . . . these are not just words, beloved, I lived the loss of virtually every aspect of my life.

Like the aftermath of a tornado, and during this hell on earth, no strong capable arms to hold us. No voice to whisper in our ear:

"Babe, it's going to be all right. We'll make it together."

Because 'together' was gone.

Forever.

And so thousands and thousands of the Father's beloved warriors find themselves literally lying on their beds, the floor, the grass, with hearts bleeding out in sheer, unadulterated pain.

Crying out to God.

Until all the tears were gone.

And the silent screaming still continued from the deepest recesses of their hearts.

Where was God's plan?

How would we survive?

When would the searing, agonizing pain ever end?

It would take a sheer miracle of God.

But miracles are often the process.

Day by day.

Night by lonely night.

Loss of purpose.

Shopping for one, not four.

Many of us moved from our beautiful homes into one-bedroom apartments.

Dreading Christmas, which used to be the happiest of times.

Complete loss of hope.

Pajamas and cats.

More pajamas.

Meds to sleep . . .

Where was the button to press to be in Heaven, away from the pain?

Pain . . . continual pain of sheer grief, abandonment and devastating loss.

And who would look after us when we were old?

When our hair was grey.

When we lost our youth.

Who would wrap us in their arms and tell us, "You're still beautiful. You are mine . . . ?"

Who would make us laugh?

. . . and who would kiss us in the rain?

How would we ever rise again, rise from the ashes, from the pain and abandonment, into beauty once more?

And so, beloved, here our seer journey with our magnificent Father begins . . .

CONVERSATION WITH THE FATHER, MINISTRY FACE-OFF

I had been hiding from the Father.

For the past three and a half years, I had been flinging myself totally on His mercy and His fellowship, but after such intense trauma, I had done everything possible to heal, received so much prayer, repented of generational lines, and received deliverance. My nature is to get help when needed . . . .to run towards healing and ministry . . . and that I'd done.

But it was as though I was stuck in a no-man's land where miracles used to come thick and furiously; it was as though I was trapped in an eternal winter.

Part of my calling in the office of the Prophet is that God uses me as Exhibit A. Shuan Boltz prophesied over me that, as a prophet, I am assigned to a generation which often means that what I experience is where many of the Body Of Christ are at that exact time.

And I knew first hand that there were so, so very many of God's champions: prophetic intercessors, prophets, seers who had been experiencing intense loss and trauma. And the valley of the shadow . . . the Wilderness.

I had stood for so long, with seemingly little hope or breakthrough, that finally I had found myself literally running away from the Father.

Deep, deep inside I knew that it was because I had cried so many tears and that I was hurting badly . . . really badly because I didn't understand why my beloved, adored Father God, my beloved Abba, who I had such a history with hadn't come to my rescue.

So I did what I did when I was a teenager . . . I ran away.

I deliberately avoided Him.

When I wasn't working on the huge deadline from my publishers regarding Book Five of *Chronicles*, I would escape into sleep and thankful oblivion or watching hours of television ... which I hadn't done for years.

But I knew that the answers weren't to be just for me ... but for so many who were going through this strange, intensive time of a seemingly unending wilderness.

I would wake up in the morning and hear Him say, 'Beloved Child' ... then I would duck my head under the blankets and run again.

But tonight was a different night.

I realized that I had to forgive God.

I had to forgive my beloved heavenly Father because the absolute truth was that I had become so intensely hurt because I felt that He had allowed me to go through so much devastating loss, that I had actually become offended by my heavenly Father. This was absolutely shocking to me because no matter what I had ever been through in my life, I had always known Him as my adored protector, my absolute rock, my all in all but this seeming 'Heaven as Brass' time threw me into a situation that seemed far above my own earthly comprehension and into a grid that I had never, never experienced before.

I was hurting so desperately and would cry out to Him like a bewildered five year old, over and over again, "I don't understand ... I don't understand ...."

"Daddy, I've served you as faithfully as I can with my whole heart all these years, bringing before you all my humanities and besetting weaknesses but if you don't come through for me, literally, I've been through so much that for the first time in my entire life, I think I'm done, Kaput, game over. I don't understand, I don't understand."

If anyone would ever have told me that there would be a time and a place where I would run from my Abba I would never have believed them.

But here I was.

Completely out of my Daddy Grid . . .

Running furiously.

And deep down, I was totally bewildered . . . and subconsciously deeply hurt and dare I say it . . . angry that I had been pushed to beyond my earthly limit . . . and the heavens were seemingly as brass.

Kim Clement had once asked God the question, 'Who is Wendy?'

And he had been so amazed by the answer that he checked and rechecked with the Father. God gave him the same answer each time:

'The Lovely Friend.'

Well . . . for sure I wasn't being the lovely friend to the Father, the lovely friend was running as fast as she could . . . away.

But I also knew that the Father had some profound truths that He wanted to share, but first I had to say 'sorry,' and ask His forgiveness and secondly, I had to stop running.

Daddy, I'm SO sorry for being so hurt and offended at you. Please forgive me. I miss you. I love you, ABBA, please help me . . . have mercy on me.

And so the Father spoke.

"Child, beloved child, I have allowed you to go through the fiery furnace that many, many of my beloved sons and daughters have been experiencing in this hour. I have allowed this because you are my scribe, and they will read your words and know deep within their hearts that they are not alone in this season of transition in the Body of Christ.

Beloved child, you and many others have been tested to almost the very limit of your endurance in this season.

For it is the season of promotion.

But the natural always follows after the spiritual . . ."

"You're saying this is an exam, Daddy?"

"Yes."

I could sense the Father's deep compassion and His smile.

"Yes, beloved weary child, it is the devil's TEST but I am the adjudicator."

"Oh, but Daddy . . . this is the severest thing I've ever experienced . . . it's taking every ounce of courage just to face the day."

Then I sensed the Father say in His infinite compassion,

"Do you remember when you sat for your final exams in High School?"

I nodded.

"For those weeks and months, normal life stopped."

I thought back. It was so true.

"So, beloved child, in that time of having to pass the exams to get your promotions, your normal activities ceased.

"Your parents put a curfew on you, so that for that season you didn't party or stay with friends and go out on the weekend.

"All the fun things you so enjoyed were put on hold. Because you had to pass the exam . . . the test.

"In this season of the Church there is a worldwide test occurring. Many are not aware of it but some of my children are.

That is why for so many in this season it has seemed that miracles are scarcer or take longer.

That is why it has seemed like winter or the wilderness.

But, beloved child . . . .Party time is ahead . . . ."

"Daddy . . . you're saying that many of us are sitting for an exam without having discerned that it is an exam?"

"Yes. You remember, when you were sitting the exam, you couldn't ask your teachers any questions?"

Complete silence.

"It was just you and the examination.

You had to literally pull on every strand of knowledge that you had learned and absorbed in that past year to see exactly what had become a part of you and what you had truly retained."

"But this, ABBA . . . this has been the hardest season for so many of us of our entire lives."

"Yes, beloved child, remember my servant Job?

Yet in the very end he received such recompense, such restitution.

I was so very proud of him. His endurance. His steadfastness. His perseverance.

He was judged by several of those who were not walking in his footsteps and who had not been called like he was in that particular season.

That is why I said, 'Do not judge.'

There is only one judge.

Beloved child, I am the only one who knows and truly understands in my infinite wisdom and compassions how intricately each child of mine has been created and the true motivation of their hearts.

I am an all-loving, omniscient, all-knowing judge.

I judge my own as a tender Father would. The reason you have felt so out of your normal grid with me is because you are not used to me being the Adjudicator."

My first instinct was to think, 'Oh, no, well, I've SO blown it!'

When the Father started to talk about courage,

"My children often think that true courage means to have no fear.

But that is not courage, beloved.

True courage is when, although having fear and having counted all the cost, you continue to walk on in endurance and faithfulness and perseverance through the fiery furnace and the burning desert wilderness clinging onto me by faith.

That is the testing of your faith in me which is more precious to me than gold.

When I look down like I looked upon my servant Job and knew that, beyond his cries, he had set his will to serve me no matter the cost.

These are my heroes of yesteryear.

These are my beloved champions of today.

My precious jewels above price.

My treasured called-out ones.

Worthy of the victor's crown.

My purple hearts."

The Father's Love.

The Father's Love.

The Father's Love.

The Father's Love.

Oh, we make Him so proud, beloved.

Even in our childish humanities and besetting sins that sometimes so easily entangle us.

And today, our incredible Father, our omniscient, omnipotent Emperor would take you in His arms and hold you to His breast and, as your tears fall upon His chest, it is He that softly, and oh, so tenderly strokes your hair and kisses your head and whispers to your tired, oh, so weary heart. "You are home, beloved . . . you are home . . . you are mine and you are truly home."

YOU CALLED ME
OUT OF DARKNESS

*H*eaven is about to invade Satan's trophy room – for you!
The mantles are being returned.

My beautiful warriors, I was reading an incredible prophetic word that declared 'the Midnight Season' is over . . . no more . . . no more . . .

And it hit my spirit so strongly.

And it was suddenly as though I had a bird's eye view of Satan's trophy room.

The demonic guards there were so complacent, they weren't even on guard. It was as though they had become so used to the literal paralysis that so, so many of the Body of Christ have found themselves living in, some for the past few years, that they were sitting scoffing, completely relaxed and off guard.

Then I was taken to a corner of the battlefield.

It was very, very dark. So dark that I could barely make out what was happening.

There were hundreds of thousands upon thousands of prisoners.

Their heads were hanging down,

Shackled.

Seemingly hopeless.

Almost like a scene from the Holocaust.

And I say their greatest treasures had been ripped from them and were being transported in huge, horse-drawn chariots to a large, dark, monstrous castle in the spirit realm.

Over these chariots I saw the words:

DREAMS.
FINANCES.
VISIONS.
HUSBANDS.
WIVES.
SONS.
INFIRMITY.
DAUGHTERS.
BUSINESSES.

There were men and women, and boys and girls, who were being transported too.

But then Satan himself came on the scene.

He was ferocious in his stance.

He rode on a monstrous steed, up and down the lines.

As though searching intently for something.

Then I saw him stop in absolute triumph.

A man was struggling violently. Satan smiled cruelly. And I heard him cry, "THE MANTLES. Rip the mantles off him!"

The man struggled valiantly but was overcome by the ferocity and outnumbered by the satanic opposition.

They wrestled a cloak from him and as it was ripped from his shoulders, I could see it was iridescent.

They threw it with huge glee and triumph on top of thousands of other mantles, scepters and crowns.

They were thrown in what seemed to be a never-ending factory line of chariots.

TO THE TROPHY ROOM!

I was then taken to a council chamber where Satan was in consultation with his princes.

They were discussing intensively how successful their strategy against the Church had been. I saw a FIVE-YEAR PLAN but it was a past plan.

One that had already been implemented.

Then the room fell silent.

And a huge bound book was placed on the table.

And somehow I knew this was the BOOK OF CHAMPIONS. God's champions.

Satan hated this book with a deep ferocity. And yet it fascinated him.

I heard them call the champions their PRIMARY TARGETS.

Many files were placed on the table and each file contained a tailor-made strategy to render those champions:

WEAK

HELPLESS

DESPAIRING

Against the champions there had been violent, brutal assignments, intricately designed to destroy the man, woman or ministry with only one goal: to steal the mantle that had been placed from Heaven upon their lives.

Satan and his council were scoffing and triumphant.

Then they walked through dark, dank corridors to what was called the Trophy Room. Satan was in his element, but as he walked towards a huge section of mantles far, far towards the back, the glory and presence exuding from them caused him intense agony.

I saw his absolute rage.

Rage at the Glory.

And I saw the word over his head:

ICHABOD. THE GLORY HAS DEPARTED.

And I realized that he feared and was in terror of the Glory.

And hated it.

Because he had lost it.

And could never, ever regain it.

Then I saw the entire Trophy Room start to shudder.

It was like a tornado.

And the most beautiful, intense, powerful, blazing light surrounded the castle.

Suddenly, Satan and his guards were paralyzed as the Trophy Room was invaded by Heaven.

It is time.

It is time to recover ALL!

And before the demons' very eyes, angels from every corner of the chamber wrested every mantle.

And I could hear the voice which made hell tremble.

It was the Father's voice.

And the Father's decree: 'IT IS ENOUGH!'

And with that the angels and the mantles disappeared.

And, I understood why so, so many minsters, why so, so many called-out ones had been almost suffocated in their callings these past months and years.

And this is the word of the Lord:

"The mantles are coming back. They are being returned."

In the coming months we will literally see ministries, families and mantles restored.

Restitution.

Beauty for Ashes.

Joy for Mourning.

Financial turnaround.

Prodigals released from bondage.

I saw a huge, dark monstrous bat like a demon be evicted over the saints and bound up. It was anxiety and fear of the future.

Take heart, beloved, beloved child of the Most High.

Your Father has just called TIME OUT on the enemy of your soul.

Oh, my beloved, darling hearts,

Take heart today.

For your KING IS COMING!

THE WOUNDED WARRIOR
LOST IN THE WOODS

For one week the Father had been telling me this story every night before I went to sleep. Every night I said to our Daddy, "Tell me the story again; tell me the story again!" The Father said that it was also for so many of you who have been lost in the 'woods' of loss, divorce, bereavement, infirmity and despair for some time now. He showed me a vision of very deep, dark woods like those in a fairy tale. The thickets and woods were so dark that it seemed that no light at all could break through. Then He took me into the deepest part of the woods and I saw a young woman, but this is YOU too! Although I could tell somehow that she had been regal and beautiful, now her hair was long, unwashed and matted, and she was dressed in rags. Her feet were bare and bleeding, and I could see she had many open sores and wounds all over her body.

But the worst was she had a spear right through her heart and, although I could tell it was a fairly old wound, it was still bleeding over her rags as though it was a fresh wound. She had been captured by a band of villains. The demonic tormentors were literally kicking her. Tormenting her. And screaming at her unrelentingly, "You're no warrior! Who do you think you are? Miss high and mighty?" The screaming would be accompanied by more kicking with big hob-nailed boots. Then they pointed in the direction far beyond the forest at a mountain far, far away and on its crest was situated the most incredible glass and crystal palace "You don't belong there!" and then another brutal kick. I saw her run away from them, tripping over large branches and landing on a pile of leaves, sobbing hysterically in desperation, her hands over her ears to keep out the voices of her tormentors. She lay on the rotting leaves for what seemed forever, clawing at them with her broken, dirty fingernails like a tormented animal. Somehow I knew that this had gone on for months and months. Then I saw another scene where she was scrabbling through the woods in some type of maze. She was becoming more and more panicked and desperate as she realized that it seemed there was no way out of her captivity.

In the third scenario, she was staring yearningly toward the palace with a half-distant memory on her face. Her head hung down and she went back into total despair. Then the Father whispered, "Now watch!"

Suddenly, there was Jesus mounted on an amazing white stallion and surrounded by his Royal Guard. Archangel Michael was among them.

Jesus led the way with his sword held high as they entered the forest.

The tormentors bowed down, trembling and terrified, unable to move.

"The Father has issued His DECREE!" Jesus' voice was soft, but filled with such authority. "We are here to return His most precious daughter and royal princess back to Him." And with that, Jesus picked up the frail, bedraggled young woman with one sweep into his strong arms,

And galloped out of the forest at top speed, headed towards the immense glass palace.

JESUS AND THE ROYAL GUARD

*J*esus, the Warrior and the Royal Guard raced out of the thickness of the forest into the open, blue sky. The Warrior winced and clasped her hands over her eyes in seeming agony. Jesus stared down tenderly and said, "It has been so long since she has known freedom and seen light that she does not know how to cope with it." He hesitated. "We must get her to the Father as quickly as possible. And bind up her wounds of which there are many." There was deep grief in his eyes. "Far too many. Our adversary has been busy."

"But, Father . . ." I interrupted the story. "How could the King's daughter . . . your daughter . . . I mean how could this happen to the Warrior?"

The Father looked at me with such patience and infinite compassion as though I was a child dull of understanding. The Father sighed deeply.

"That girl is YOU. That girl is many, many of those who are reading this parable today." I stared at the suffering princess in horror.

And I knew that this had indeed been me and many other precious ones, caught in the woods of devastating circumstances that had threatened to shackle us and take us captive. I knew to be quiet and listen to the rest of the story.

Jesus and the Royal Guard raced across the wastelands and were halfway to the glistening palace when an immense light overshadowed the entire terrain.

Slowly, ever so slowly, the wounded princess raised her head, "Father," she uttered in wonder. Then her head fell upon her bruised chest.

"It can't be," she murmured. "I have failed Him so."

And tears streamed down her grimy cheeks, falling onto her bruised and battered fingers. "I have failed my Father and my King . . ."

But the immense, pulsating and blinding compassionate light drew nearer and nearer until the angels of the Royal Guard dismounted from their horses and fell onto their faces. And Jesus dropped to his knees in the wake of the magnificent, omniscient mercies emanating from the Father.

"Father!" Jesus uttered, "Abba!" And he walked into the midst of the bright, pulsating light. Then suddenly a great silence fell.

If ever a silence could be deep . . . filled with tender mercies and compassion.

It was the very presence of the Father.

And out of the midst of the light and the rainbow walked an immense form.

And as the form drew nearer the warrior, who was now lying on the ground, shaking, the being became almost the form of a man . . . and yet not of a man . . . it was the Father . . . And very slowly the Father knelt, His eyes fixed on one thing only . . . His wounded, sobbing daughter. He took her face in His hands and kissed her matted hair over and over again.

And then He held her so fiercely to His breast that it was as though He would never, ever let her go. The spear in her heart literally dissolved to pieces in the wake of the Father's love.

And slowly she mustered up the courage to raise her head.

She opened her eyes. And slowly recognition dawned.

"Daddy!"

The Father stared down at her with such infinite yearning.

Such infinite kindness and goodness and the understanding of the ages.

And His tears mingled with hers as they fell on her matted hair.

"Daddy, I thought you would never find me . . . ," the warrior sobbed. "I failed you so badly . . . they told me . . ."

"They told you lies, beloved. They attacked, stole and ransacked all you held dear, then in your anguish they kidnapped you into their kingdom.

"They lied to you and told you that you did not belong in the palace.

"That I, the King, was not your Father. The tormentors wore you down until you lost your identity as my child. As my daughter." Tears streamed down the Father's face. "YOU are the reason I sent my Son to Calvary. You are the love . . . the light of my being. The adversary has targeted my princes and princesses, my precious sons and daughters, in order to break my heart. For I cannot bear to see you in such pain and agony.

"In this present age he has targeted many of my greatly beloved sons and daughters with the devastating rejection and betrayal of divorce; he has stolen wives, husbands and sons and daughters from them in death; he has bound their limbs and bodies in physical pain and disease; he has inflicted such mental, emotional and physical suffering upon them that they literally could not face the day. And lost their will to fight. Then they lost the will to live. But enough of that for now."

The Father lifted His warrior in His arms and started toward the palace. "Make haste!" He cried "My daughter, my royal princess, has been badly wounded and tortured by the enemy, we must heal her wounds! For she will rise again STRONGER and WISER and deal a devastating death blow to the enemy's camp but not until she is fully healed . . ."

And I watched as the Father carried His precious daughter, His princess, towards the great doors of the palace.

Father and daughter could literally not take their eyes off of one another. Jesus looked at me. "She has come home. She is back with the lover of her soul. She is back with her Father. Now her healing will begin . . ."

PROPHETIC SEER INTERPRETATION OF WOUNDED WARRIORS IN THE WOODS

UNLEASHING OF LUST, SEDUCTION AND JEZEBEL, ABANDONMENT, REJECTION, ANXIETY, DESPAIR . . .

For every one of the Father's beloved, precious sons and daughters who have found themselves in the woods . . .

I said, "Daddy, how did the warrior who was your adored daughter end up being tormented by the enemy in the forest?"

I heard the Father say, "The princess is a picture of so many, many of my beloved sons and daughters in the Earth at this time."

I could feel the great compassion and tender mercy in His voice . . .

"So many of my sons and daughters ruled and reigned with me for many years, walked with me intimately, prayed for many.

"Worshipped me in the secret place . . . knew peace.

"Knew my presence.

"Ministered for me.

"The enemy well knew that these were my treasures.

"That I delighted in them.

"That they sat at my table,

"And were my joy.

"But in this past season, a great and violent onslaught was issued from the bowels of hell itself.

"An onslaught intricately designed to shake some of those who were closest to me, the ones I called friend, to shake them to their very core."

I asked, "Daddy, was our hedge of protection down?"

Again, I sensed such compassion.

"Beloved, none of my children are perfect. Yes, there were certain areas in my sons' and daughters' lives that were unguarded, but I covered you.

"But this past season has been a season of transition,

"A season of shift.

"A season where the old and comfortable had to make way for the new, and the new wineskin, for the old wineskin would have burst in many of my children's lives.

"The old foundation was not strong enough to stand the weight of what so many of my daughters and sons are being called out to in the next season.

"The enemy asked in this dispensation to sift many, many of those who walked in intimacy with me.

"To sift many of those who called me friend and Father.

"And a great unleashing of the spirit of LOSS and ABANDON-MENT, a great unleashing of the Jezebelic spirit was released against marriages, families. There have been many casualties. Husbands seduced away from the wives of their youth. Sons and daughters lost in death and addiction. Businesses and ministries lost. And a spirit of chaos was released from hell."

Suddenly, as the Father was talking, the heavens opened up and I saw a vast battlefield in front of me.

It was a terrible sight.

What once had been a mighty army of both men and women (but the Lord zoomed in on the women now).

And I saw the before picture.

These mighty, powerful warriors, now all marching in formation with their heads held high.

But ahead, unseen around a corner, the enemy was waiting soundlessly.

It seemed as though there were thousands of snipers who had been trained with deadly accuracy.

Then I saw princes of hell in a crypt-like chamber, studying literally thousands of these princess warriors' blueprints.

They were poring over them, going back through generational lines,

Studying their wives and husbands, their children.

Searching for legal entry points. This was no small task and it seemed that it had been intricately planned by the enemy specifically for THIS season, against this certain dispensation of warrior princess fighters, who were earmarked to do mighty exploits for the Kingdom of God in the soon-coming season.

I sensed the enemy's fear of these wounded warriors.

Many of the men and women were prophetic intercessors.

Many, many, prayed.

Others were powerful ministers, unknown to man but known to Heaven.

I overheard one scheming demon who was frustrated as he studied the blueprints declare triumphantly,

"The husbands! Entice the husbands with the SPIRIT OF LUST, SEDUCTION and JEZEBEL . . . And the woman will crumble!"

And I saw a major onslaught planned in the second heaven to launch an assault on many of these men who had unhealed 'Father' wounds, an orphan spirit or one who had never closed the door completely on the spirit of lust.

I saw demonic riders being released to war against men, carrying banners that read:

SPIRIT OF LUST,

SEDUCTION,

And JEZEBEL.

And I heard a great demonic roar saying:

"TAKE THEIR COVERING DOWN!"

And then there was a second set of riders released.

They were released against the women,

And on these banners was written:

LOSS

REJECTION

ABANDONMENT

DESPAIR

PANIC ATTACKS

ADDICTION

SUICIDE

And they followed behind the first set of riders.

The next vision I had was once again back to the vast battleground.

But where before there had been powerful marching warriors, now thousands of beautiful, noble men and women were lying on the ground literally writhing in agony, wounded and bleeding.

Many of them had spears and swords straight through their hearts.

And I saw the word from the Enemy's camp:

BULL'S EYE.

And a great host of Heaven was released to minister to these men and women

But, and this was the hard thing to watch, many of them could not only not receive the angelic help, but were so delirious that even the seers who had been hit were having difficulty recognizing the angelic help.

And no matter how they tried, so many of these men and women were in such pain, trying desperately to stop their own bleeding and bind up their own wounds, they literally could not get up.

THE BATTLEGROUND

I looked in terrible distress at these previously beautiful, noble, mighty warriors. Their bodies were literally strewn across the battlefield as far as the eye could see. I saw the words:

INFIRMITY-DEBILITATION-DEATH-LOSS.

But the majority of the warriors were unable to get up, because the largest number of them were bleeding profusely from spears and swords that had impaled them directly through their hearts. I saw several stagger to their feet but they were immediately overtaken with the next banner I saw – GRIEF – and fell like lead back onto the ground again. The sound of sobbing. The sound of utter, agonized wailing was spine-chilling. There were desperate agonized cries of "Jesus! Jesus!"

And screams of agony as some wrestled with all their might to pull the swords and spears out of their own hearts with little or no success at all.

Those who had walked in strength, courage and valor for years were as weak as babes. There was no will to arise. There was no strength to arise. Warrior after warrior lay among their brothers and sisters on the battlefield and I saw the words:

TRUAMA-SHOCK-LOSS-DEVASTATION-GRIEF-
REJECTION-ABANDONMENT.

And the largest banner of all, which seemed to echo the cry from the wounded warriors:

NO WILL TO LIVE.

Then from the rear was released a huge entourage of nurses who I somehow knew to be loyal, faithful, praying friends and family, lovingly tending their wounded. But however much love, however much anointing, these ones tenderly poured on them it was as though nothing was healing their wounds.

As soon as the bandages were applied, the bleeding started again.

Many of the wounded thrust them away and turned their heads into the dirt muttering, "I have no reason to live." The nurses began to be filled with consternation. Then a group of matrons arrived but they did not deal as gently with them as the nurses had. I saw many of the matrons literally attempt to force the wounded up and they became angry when the wounded warriors staggered a few steps, then fell back into the blood and dirt. I overheard a couple of matrons complaining loudly,

"What's the matter with them? They should be walking by now."

Then they shouted. "GET UP! GET UP! GET UP!"

"It's self-pity," another said, and then she pulled one beautiful, bloodied warrior with matted hair to their feet.

"Walk!" she commanded. But the warrior was so weak and had no will to put one foot in front of the other. The matrons were confounded.

Then the doctors arrived. They were diagnosticians.

They waved the matrons away and examined the wounded.

Then they gathered together, whispering in consternation, "We have to remove the swords and spears. If heart surgery is not done, these wounded warriors will not recover." The head doctor spoke quietly. He was WISDOM. "These noble, valiant warriors have taken a direct hit to their hearts. Out of the heart flow the ISSUES OF LIFE. The issues of life are rapidly pouring from their wounds." He turned to the matrons in a stern manner, "This was NOT because these warriors failed to guard their hearts.

"Many of these you see here are unrecognizable. For they were warriors. Unafraid. Courageous. Steadfast. These wounds have been inflicted by the enemy because they became dangerous to him, not by their own folly.

"Treat them with the honor they are due, for the King is on His way

"And they shall be healed. And they shall arise as mighty warriors in His End-Time Harvest." And the doctors turned into a host of healing angels.

And each wounded warrior was assigned at least four or five angels.

And the angels were pouring out healing balm on their wounds.

Time passed and this time the balm started to take effect.

Then suddenly the most incredible blazing light overshadowed the battlefield. It caught every warrior's attention.

And for the first time they became cognizant.

Many stretched out their hands towards the light.

And as the light came nearer, Jesus, adorned in royal robes and

wearing a crown bearing the title 'KING OF KINGS,' rode a white charger.

He was weeping. And as he wept, it was as though a great rush of compassion erupted from his heart. It was in the form of light rays and the rays started to settle, almost hover, over each broken heart.

And a host of angelic messengers were carrying banners that read:

SUPERNATURAL HEALING OF MIND, EMOTIONS
AND SOUL.

And for the first time, I saw incredible hope rise up in many of the wounded warriors. Jesus dismounted and started towards the nearest warrior. He gently, oh, so tenderly sat them up, wiped their brow and took their bloodied face in his hands. Their eyes, which had been dull and unseeing, suddenly cleared in recognition of the King. And Jesus cupped their face in his hands, looking on them with incomparable love. And I watched in awe as the sword through their heart slowly dissolved.

And then I saw THE LION, and a great and terrible awe and fear and incredible hope swept through the battlefield and the chant swelled: "LION IS COMING! THE LION IS COMING!"

THE LION ROARS

*A*nd, as THE LION came . . . as He surveyed the battle-field, He started to roar, and in His roar was DIVINE JUDGMENT against the enemy.

And in His roar was DIVINE WRATH against the shackles that had imprisoned His warriors' hearts and minds.

And as He roared, I saw mists of hopelessness and desperation, depression and despair and infirmity consumed into ashes by His all-consuming fire. And I saw iron shackles and what looked to be medieval instruments of torture that had literally been binding many of the wounded who were lying bleeding on the battlefield shatter. Shatter like glass into thousands of fragments. And a terrible screaming and shrieking erupted from the demon tormentors. And I saw thousands upon thousands of dark, demonic entities like bats with talons rise in utter terror into the skies overhead and flee with all their might.

And still the Lion roared. And in His roar was JUSTICE.

And in His roar was REDEMPTION. And in His roar was RESTORATION. And in His roar was RESTITUTION.

And in His roar were terrible tears and terrible grieving.

And He breathed yet again over His wounded warriors.

And, as the consuming fire of His all-consuming LOVE and PRESENCE poured over them, one by one, it was as though a mist departed from them and they woke as though out of a dream. And I saw thousands of healing angels released, ministering a holy anointing balm to the wounded hearts.

And the vials of balm all had the same label and, on the label was written one word: HOPE. And as the balm of hope was administered, a second terrible screaming erupted, but this time it was a wave of darkness that had been lodged deep, so deep in their wounded hearts.

And the healing balm dislodged the tormenting spirits that were buried deep in their wounded hearts, minds, wills and emotions. And these spirits flew out at the speed of light in utter torment. And the spirits' names were:

HOPE DEFERRED. And then the Lion roared once more and in the fire from His roar was written: HOPE AND A FUTURE.

FAITH RESTORED. And on banners all across the battlefield I saw the words: SUDDENLY, SUDDENLY. Then the Lion roared again and in His roar was RENEWED HOPE and FAITH. And miracles began to break out all across the battlefield. And then the Lion transformed into the Father.

And the Father spoke: "My sons and daughters for a long while have been imprisoned in winter, but the spring has come and the summer draws quickly nigh . . ." And then He raised His mighty scepter and decreed in a voice of ten thousand waters: "PREPARE FOR SUDDENLIES!

"PREPARE FOR SUDDENLIES! Tokens in the land of the living.

"Divine shifts in circumstances. Overnight healings. Desires of the heart released. Creative Miracles. Restitutions. Engagement Rings. Weddings.

"Prodigals Returning. Families Reunited. Financial Miracles. Ruths appearing. Boazes arriving. Lack broken. Legacies released. Court cases settled. Contracts signed and sealed. Spouses returning. Infirmities broken. PREPARE FOR THE SUDDENLIES OF THE MOST HIGH GOD."

PROPHETIC WORD – DON'T LIE DOWN ON THE BATTLEFIELD

Beloved Warriors,

I was in America traveling and I had been dealing with immense pressure.

But the Father literally HIT my spirit and told me that this is an incredibly urgent, and for some, a literally life-or-death word:

"My child, beloved child, even in the profound weakness and raging battle you find yourself in this very moment, lift your ear to me and hear what I have to say.

"You have fallen in complete weariness.

"I watched as you sank to your knees, overcome with despair after standing in faith for so long, and as you fell to your knees, the enemy of your soul aimed straight at your most vulnerable place in your arsenal: your heart.

"And it was a direct hit, my child, and you fell on the battlefield.

"Oh, beloved, beloved child of my heart, I watched, as in your pain and total weariness from the battle from months upon months of the fiercest warfare you have ever experienced, you laid down on the battlefield, in the midst of the raging battle, and closed your eyes.

"Sleep. Sleep . . ."

"Then crying, 'Father, I cannot face the battle anymore. I am knocked out. Let me sleep. The sleep of escape.'

"And for a short moment you felt rest.

"But still the battle was raging all around you.

"But you could not bear to open your eyes or find the strength to rise to your feet. 'Let me sleep on the battlefield.'

"And Heaven was alerted, for, although sleep was sweet and it was a brief escape, Heaven knew that it was an enticement and an entrapment and that if you did not arise, you would be overcome by the enemy while you slept.

"Oh, child,

"I am talking to you, oh, so beloved weary, weary one.

"You who have cried to me."

I replied, "Father, this is it, I am done.

"I am finished.

"I have nothing left.

"No might.

"No strength.

"No ability to face the day."

The Father was determined,

"But I tell you now, my child, my angelic forces have been released and are hurrying to your side.

"Jesus, oh, great Lover of your soul, is riding toward you on his great white charger.

"Your King is coming, your King is coming."

And the cry from Heaven rang out:

"NEVER lie down on the battlefield in the midst of the battle.

"When you feel you are falling, cry out to Heaven, for Heaven hears.

"Cry out to Jesus, for Jesus hears."

Beloved, I watched as Jesus picked up the ones who were lying weary and completely unable to help themselves.

Oh, how tenderly he held and kissed their forehead and gently removed the spear from their heart.

Then, as their eyes flickered open, although they had so very little strength, they smiled through their tears in relief at the lover of their soul.

"Never lie down on the battlefield," Jesus whispered.

"When your strength to fight seems gone,

"And you are so weary that you feel yourself falling in the battle,

"Cry to me.

"For I will come directly to your aid.

"My child,

"I was in Gethsemane.

"I am deeply, deeply moved and touched by your infirmities.

"Oh child, beloved child, I too have known the agony of abandonment.

"Of betrayal.

"Of misunderstanding.

"Of agonizing loss.

"I will never leave you nor forsake you.

"Never.

"Never.

"I am he who is true."

And I watched as Jesus placed the tired, wounded, weary one on his steed, and as they leant their head on his back as he rode to the front of the battle.

And as they rode, they passed angelic hosts with oils and liniments who rode alongside and ministered to the wounded warriors' hearts and minds.

And slowly they regained their strength until by the time they reached the front lines, they were riding the steed themselves with their heads held high,

And brandishing their swords.

And Jesus was gone.

Oh, Father, I release supernatural strength for the battle to all who have lain down in the midst of the raging war on the battlefield.

Beloved Jesus, come to our aid.

Strengthen, encourage, minister as only you can.

I release in the spirit realm divine hope to the hopeless.

Divine freedom to the captive.

Divine strength to the weary.

"RISE UP. RISE UP, beloved," Jesus cries. "You are nearly through transition, you are so close. Don't lie down on the battlefield now when you are so close to victory.

"I AM your strength.

"I AM your future.

"I AM your purpose.

"I AM your deliverer.

"You shall surely see my goodness in the land of the living. Your harvest is upon you.

"Yes, for many of you, like Peter, the enemy asked for you, that you may be sifted. But we have prayed for you, that your faith would not fail. The process of sifting is almost over; at an end. And the glory.

"The victor's crown.

"The harvest.

"An incredible harvest awaits you.

"All things restored.

"Nothing lost.

"Restitution.

"Restoration.

"The oil of joy for mourning.

"Hold on through the last of the storm for, beloved child of my heart, the shore is now in sight."

Love, your Abba Father

THE TORTURE CHAMBER

*T*hose who know me will understand that I do intensive research when I write the Chronicles of Brothers series.

Some of this research entailed studying torture methods in Black Ops sites.

It was then that the Father said to me,

'Wendy . . . It is of the utmost importance that my sons and daughters need to gain understanding and discernment on the reason for the seemingly barren season that they have been walking through.'

Then the Father explained to me that many of us who are His called out ones marked for great exploits in this next dispensation have been marching on the frontline of his great army.

In this present season the enemy of our souls stepped up his strategies and warfare to a degree that was so intensely violent and ruthless and many were taken as prisoners of war.

Not because you failed him . . .

Not because you were weak and sometimes stumbling . . .

But because from Heaven's viewpoint you were the Father's beloved champions and were specifically targeted by the enemy with tailor-made assignments designed to literally break you.

In our modern world torture is designed to break the soldiers' mind, will and emotions . . . their soul . . . by lies, intense manipulation of the facts, isolation and disorientation.

And to break your physical resilience by pushing your mind and body to the maximum breaking point . . . until you have lost all will to live and feel you are losing your mind.

The deprivation tactics include holding out reward or hope, then taking it away . . . driving the POW to desperation and despair.

But the primary goal is total loss of hope . . .

No one knows their coordinates. No one is coming to rescue them.

TOTAL AND UTTER DESPAIR, LOSS OF ALL HOPE AND A BLEAK FUTURE . . .

And with that the prisoner has lost the one thing that could keep him resilient and he succumbs to the captor's lies.

They are often blindfolded, a fear tactic, loss of orientation, or bombarded day and night with light and sound, depriving them of sleep . . . again disorientation.

Then, in their disorientated, weakened state, they are questioned and physically tortured until their body and mind are at breaking point.

And they are told over and over again that no one is coming to rescue them . . .

Threats against the dearest in their life . . . you'll never see your wife and children again.

Until HOPE is completely destroyed.

And so it has been for so many ordinary people in this past season.

The loss of businesses, homes, marriages, divorce, the death of spouses and sons or daughters, the loss of finances, and loss of ministries have led many, many of us into isolation, disorientation and despair.

We have cried out to the Father who always ran to our aid . . . but the miracles are few . . . Heaven seems so silent . . .

You have been tested by the enemy.

NOT because you are weak but because you are STRONG.

You were put on the frontline because through the years you trained for the elite 'SAS' or 'DELTA FORCE.'

You were chosen by Heaven because of your faithfulness, your unswerving devotion to Jesus, the Father and His cause.

Your history with God moved Heaven . . .

You walked in obedience . . . in faithfulness . . . in courage unwavering.

Then the heat turned up.

No one truly knows what Joseph experienced in prison.

The Psalms give us a glimpse of David's agony in Ziglag when his own team wanted to turn against him, their homes were razed to the dust, their women and children taken.

David was called and ordained to be King of Israel yet he cried out in agony to the Lord, running from Saul hiding in Adullum in Ziglag. BUT FOR OUR MIGHTY GOD. If David and Joseph and Daniel and Abraham had given up, pressed completely beyond their endurance . . . they would not have become King of Israel, 2nd in command to Pharaoh . . . Father of Nations . . .

And when our Lord Jesus cried out, agonized, sweating blood in Gethsemane . . . crying on the cross: '*Eloi Eloi Sabacthani . . . My God, My God, why have you forsaken me?*' If he had aborted the greatest mission of all time when he was tortured and deserted and disorientated and the greatest love of his life appeared to have forsaken him . . . the consequences are unthinkable.

That is why in Scripture Paul exhorts us to endurance and perseverance.

NOT ONLY SO, BUT WE ALSO GLORY IN OUR SUFFERINGS, BECAUSE WE KNOW THAT SUFFERING PRODUCES PERSEVERANCE; PERSEVERANCE, CHARACTER; AND CHARACTER, HOPE. AND HOPE DOES NOT PUT US TO SHAME, BECAUSE GOD'S LOVE HAS BEEN

POURED OUT INTO OUR HEARTS THROUGH THE HOLY SPIRIT, WHO

HAS BEEN GIVEN TO US.

(Romans 5:3–5 NIV)

The Father has NOT forgotten you.

Right now, the angelic host have been assigned your exact co-ordinates . . . Heaven has been deeply moved by your faithfulness, your endurance, your steadfastness under immense duress and the elite force of Heaven under Archangel Michael's command are under direct orders to come to your aid.

They have been instructed to care for you;

To heal your mind and heart;

To roll away the tombstone;

To remove every delay, diversion and deferral of your call and dreams.

God is on the move.

And He is about to hand out PURPLE HEARTS.

Your Purple Heart, beloved . . .

The Purple Heart is a United States military decoration awarded in the name of the President to those wounded or killed while serving and in combat.

The army honors its wounded.

And so does Heaven.

If we only understood how greatly you are esteemed and honored by the Father and Jesus . . . it is a holy sacred mandate.

Oh . . . how proud the Father is of you.

Oh, so courageous one,

You have stood the test,

The prison doors are open,

Your captors are in chains.

As you walk out into the sunlight,
Hear the mighty roar of Heaven's cloud of witnesses . . .
"Well done . . . good and faithful servant . . .
Well done . . ."

YOU ARE BEAUTIFUL

*Y*ou are so beautiful, beloved friend.

You are beautiful in your uniqueness. How the Father took such intricate care in forming every facet of your being.

You are so beautiful.

He chose the family you were birthed into and He knows the number of hairs upon your head.

He formed you while you were still in your mother's womb.

You were so fearfully and wonderfully made.

He looked down upon you and whispered,

"This child is my delight,

"My song,

"My joy."

Oh, how He loves you.

Oh, how infinitely treasured you are by Him.

And, oh . . . how incredibly beautiful you are.

Beloved Father, I bring your beautiful child before you today and I ask you in the name of Jesus to encounter them in a way in which they have never known you before.

In the name of Jesus, I release Holy Spirit visitation upon their life. Holy Spirit visitation, Holy Spirit encounter.

Dreams in the night. Visions in the day.

I release the seer anointing to enable them to see.

The presence of His Holy Spirit overwhelming you with the Father's love.

Oh, Father, I release your love to this precious one's heart.

I release your mercy.

O Father, encounter this hungry one's heart. Where their heart has been hungry and dry, where they have cried out for a tangible anointing of your presence, let your presence come.

Where they have cried out for the supernatural, let the supernatural flow.

Where they have cried out to see your hand in the land of the living, thank you for the release of a special token of your love and your compassions upon them today.

Thank you, Father. We decree a release of divine encouragement, a release of supernatural favor into every circumstance of their lives.

YOU ARE BEAUTIFUL

Child, you are beautiful to me.

Even in your times of uncertainty and self- rejection you are beautiful to me.

For I am the one who chose you before your conception.

I am the one who knew every facet of your soul.

I am the one who created you so intricately in your inward parts. Every emotion, every weakness, every incredible strength that I placed inside you. I find you to be beautiful.

And, yes, beloved, in this past season there have been many, many times when the enemy has sought to deface you and write his own destiny and future for you on your soul, but remember, beloved child of my heart, I AM with you.

There is nothing, nothing, nothing that can remove you from my hand, because your heart is so toward me.

Know this, that even in your very frailest and weakest of times, when I hear you whisper, "Daddy,"

I run to the very sound of your cry,

And I, the God of Israel,

I, the God of your hard places,

I, the God who formed you and framed you,

I am moved.

Oh, my child,

I am so moved by your faith in me.

When the enemy has come in like a flood and you have felt the violent onslaught of his attack and yet you have clung to me even in your weakest of times.

That, beloved, has touched my heart, for that is faith indeed.

So, lift up your eyes, weary child, lift up your gaze to my eyes and reach out your hand to me.

And know that it is I who sees and that I am your rewarder, for you shall yet see my goodness in the land of the living.

And every promise that I have given you shall not be robbed from you, beloved son, beloved daughter, for YOU are mine.

YOU are mine.

You are mine.

O Father, encounter this hungry one's heart. Where their heart has been hungry and dry, where they have cried out for a tangible anointing of your presence, let your presence come.

Where they have cried out for the supernatural, let the supernatural flow.

Where they have cried out to see your hand in the land of the living, thank you for the release of a special token of your love and your compassions upon them today.

Thank you, Father. We decree a release of divine encouragement, a release of supernatural favor into every circumstance of their lives.

He loves you!

THE YELLOW BRICK ROAD.
HOPE DEFERRED NO MORE.

Beloved Warriors,

A few days ago, the Holy Spirit kept putting in my spirit the yellow brick road from "The Wizard of Oz."

I asked the Father, "Why?"

He showed me a vision of thousands of men and women, but mainly women, on a yellow brick road. They were exhausted, some stumbling and falling. Many were helping each other up as they continued toward the palace far, far away.

Then the Father brought to my remembrance the time when I had gone to see "The Wizard of Oz" when I was little, and I was so desperate to see God in the palace, that when it turned out that it was just a man who was there, I remember my little-girl heart being devastated with disappointment.

Then the Father said,

"You thought you were going to see me . . . ?"

"Yes, Daddy . . ."

Oh, even at that young age, I thought there would be the mighty Emperor at the end of the road . . . God himself.

I never forgot the terrible disappointment I felt.

Then the Father said,

"You see all these thousands upon thousands of men and women completely exhausted, struggling to put one foot in front of the other?

Then the Wicked Witch with the green face (I was terrified of her when I was little) kept swooping down across the yellow brick road.

And the Father said,

"This is my Yellow Brick Road

"And at the end is my rainbow, representing all the good promises I have given my children.

"RESTITUTION,

"RESTORATION,

"HOPE,

"HEALING.

"NO MORE HOPE DEFERRED.

"For my kingdom is not a delusion and deception as in "The Wizard of Oz," but, as my sons and daughters stay fixed on My path during some of the most intense warfare and battles of their lives, as they near the end of the road, they will discover:

"My presence.

"My Glory.

"My promises.

"Everything that has been stolen is at the end of my rainbow.

"And within my Throne room.

"For my rainbow does not offer false hope and delusion,

"But truth and peace for the weary heart.

"Restoration of every dream.

"And every material thing that the enemy has stolen from them in this past season of violent warfare."

And in the overarching rainbow these words were written:

"NO MORE HOPE DEFERRED."

And the palace was the Throne Room.

I saw myriads of ministering angels greeting those that finally made it.

And their feet were anointed and washed.

Old garments were removed, new mantels and robes were placed on them.

And crowns and scepters were handed out, for they were kings.

And a great cry arose from the Throne Room.

"Enough is enough; it is now payback time."

And I saw the enemy's plunder taken by angelic formations and mighty, mighty restitution was taking place.

THE BAGGAGE

There were thousands and thousands of men, women and children stumbling through a vast wilderness. It was almost like a scene from the Holocaust.

Every person was either hauling such heavy baggage or pushing carts which seemed to hold their entire life possessions.

Each was clinging desperately to what was theirs, stumbling through valleys and ravines. Far, far ahead was the most incredible, glistening, azure sea. And Jesus was standing with inexpressible joy at the sea's edge.

Eventually an old woman reached the edge of the sea and Jesus gently, held out his hands to the woman.

She was dressed in rags and holding on for dear life to an urn. She could not let go of it. Jesus looked at her and loved her.

"It is a new season," he said gently "And a new wineskin.

"You have carried this urn all through the wilderness and the season of transition, but it is your sustenance no longer."

Very gently he removed the urn from the old woman's grasp.

She clawed at it desperately. Everyone watched in silence as Jesus emptied the contents of the urn upon the ground. It was full of ashes.

The woman cried in desperation. "You have known hope deferred for so long," Jesus said tenderly, "that you have carried your broken heart with you too scared to lose control again. Scared that surrender only meant more heartache . . ." Then he smiled the most brilliant of smiles.

"But this is what I meant when I said, 'BEAUTY FOR ASHES!'"

And Jesus removed from another urn the most dazzling, exquisite jewels of iridescent hues and poured them into her trembling, out-stretched hands.

The crowd gasped, but not so much at the jewels, but at the transformation taking place in the old woman. Her greyed hair became thick and long and dark and glossy again. Her face was young and shining with hope.

Jesus nodded. And two angels clothed her in royal robes.

Jesus placed a tiara upon her head, then gently kissed her forehead.

"Surrender . . . surrender, beloved, is the key to freedom, exchange your baggage for mine, for my yoke is easy and my burden is light . . ."

Dearly beloved, I bring you, so intricately and wonderfully made before our wonderful Father in Heaven.

Father, I ask you in the name of Jesus Christ, your beloved Son, that no matter what this precious one has faced this past year, the wind of your Holy Spirit would blow like a fresh wind over their soul, restoring their mind and their will and healing their emotions from the long period of faithfully walking through the wilderness.

COURAGE – A NEW SEASON

*C*ourageous one, reading these very pages.

Courageous one, you who have walked through the driest of wildernesses. Through the storm and the waters that so many times threatened to overtake you. It is to you that I speak today.

And yet you say,

"But, Father, I have no courage.

"I have been so weak.

"I have almost lost my way."

And the Father would say to you, so deeply moved,

"My child, beloved child,

"When in your greatest moments of weakness and humanity in your deepest, almost unbearable, moments, when the pain of life and all that assailed you threatened to overwhelm you,

"Still you stood.

"Yet still, with tears coursing down your face,

"You would whisper, 'Jesus, Jesus.'

"I ran to your side.

"And I lifted you into my arms, into my tender embrace, and I carried you.

"And my own tears mingled with your tears as I watched you while you slept, so weary from the warfare you encountered, and I whispered over you:

"Courage. Courage.

"This is my courageous child.

"Oh, how you moved my heart.

"For even in your deepest grief, you stood steadfast in your heart

"And cried, 'Father.'

"And when you could not pray,

"I heard your cry.

"You never forsook me, my beloved one.

"And, as I watched you stand when you were too weary to fight,

"Yet, still you stood even in your times of greatest pain and greatest fear.

"That is courage indeed.

"And the whole of Heaven watched as you clung to me,

"Your heart still towards me.

"Your cry still to serve me.

"Oh, how you moved Heaven; oh, greatly beloved.

"But, the storm is passing, my child.

"The storm that was assigned against your life by the enemy is passing.

"For I, the great I AM, am rising on your behalf.

"Enough!

"My eyes are ever upon you.

"Your life's scroll is before me.

"My angelic host are moving on your behalf.

"Just one more step, my beloved.

"For surely you shall see my GOODNESS in the land of the living,

"And every dream that has seemed so far gone shall be restored to you.

"A new season is upon you, child. And a new time."

A NEW SEASON

"Fresh wind . . . fresh wind . . . fresh wind," says the Holy Spirit.

"I am about to release the wind of Heaven upon your mind, upon your body, upon your emotions . . .

"A fresh wind that blows away the old and beckons in the new . . .

"A fresh wind that blows away the heaviness of the warring years, and overshadows you with hope and joy . . .

"With peace that passes your understanding.

"For I am imparting fresh vision," says the Lord.

"I am imparting fresh vision to your heart.

"Dreams that have been deferred.

"Hope that was lost.

"The wilderness that seemed not to bloom.

"Behold, I come, my child.

"I come as the King of Heaven, I come as your King, I come in my glory . . .

"I come in my majesty . . . I come in my power . . .

"To change the course of the winds that have been blowing over your life.

"And where you have seen wilderness, the rose will bloom.

"And where your land has been a dry and thirsty land, rivers, rushing rivers, shall flow over your heart, over your soul, over your circumstances . . .

"Washing away the dust of yesteryear . . .

"Healing disappointments and restoring the breaches of your heart . . .

"For in this new year, I shall show myself to be the restorer of your "breach. Restorer of your heart. Restorer of your body.

"Restorer of your finances.

"Restorer of your dreams . . ."

Father, I release your Holy Spirit over this life in the name of Jesus.

Heal that which could not be healed.

Restore that which could not be restored.

Resurrect that which they said could not live.

Pour out your consuming love, your unending mercies, upon your beloved son, your beloved daughter, each day,

That they might know the height, depth, and breadth of your love for them.

That they might find refuge in your strong arms even as a babe does with its earthly father,

For you are the Father from whom all fatherhood was named.

The most beautiful.

The most compassionate of whose understanding there is no end.

Our glorious Father.

HE LOVES YOU!

THE SEASON OF TRANSITION

*O*h, Father,

  Today I pray for all who have been in a period of transition,

For those of your heart who have cried out,

"Will this wilderness, this dry and arid place, never end?"

"Oh, beloved son, beloved daughter,

"Be not amazed by the seemingly fiery trial, but know this

"That many, many, in this season have been in a period of transition.

"Transition is the most painful time of a mother giving birth.

"Just before the baby's head crowns,

"Just before the ultimate joy of birth.

"Hold on. Hold on.

"You are nearly through.

"The light at the end of the tunnel comes far closer, and soon you will be thrust into a brand-new day of restoration and restitution where all things are made new.

"Hold on. Hold on, weary, war-torn, beloved child, for a new song will be upon your lips, as you transition into every dream, every appointed vision, and everything written in your life's scroll since before the beginning of time.

"Your shift is nigh upon you."

SHIFTING FROM TRANSITION

"*C*hild, beloved child of my heart,

"You have been in a season of transition.

"You have been in a season where the autumn leaves have dropped from the branches and you have been left staring in bewilderment and confusion at the bare branches of the winter season."

"'But, Father,' you have cried out to me. 'Father, Father, I have sowed so much. I have tried with every fiber of my heart to be faithful.'"

"And yet, as you look around at your life all that is visible to you in this transition season before winter transforms into spring, is the stripping and the desolation of dreams that seem aborted and a destiny that was sovereignly ordained even before your conception.

And you stare helplessly at the barrenness."

"But I say to you this day and in this hour, my beloved son, my beloved daughter, lift, lift up your eyes.

"Lift your eyes above the bare branches.

"Lift, lift your gaze above the barrenness.

"For your redemption draws nigh.

"And, even in a breath, beloved, the bare branches will start to bud again.

"And even in the midst of the seemingly fiery wilderness, lilies and the rose of Sharon shall bloom again.

"But this coming season is not like before, my child.

"Yesteryear was a season of childish things but today is a season when the fire and the ferocious storm have molded you in preparation for a different day.

"A day of courage and tenacity.

"A day of endurance.

"For it is in this fiery furnace that you have counted the cost.

"And, I saw in the midnight hour when you cried out to me in your seeming anguish, 'I cannot pay this price.'"

"And yet even as the tears streamed down your face, still I heard your whisper, 'Father, I will still serve you.'

"And now know this, beloved one, you have been counted faithful.

"You have passed the test of the enemy.

"Your spring is upon you. The buds are already blooming far above your gaze.

"And now, beloved, I will take you by my strong right hand and lead you and guide you through the last of the rocky places, into your promised land.

"So, lift your weary head, my child.

"Strengthen the feeble eyes, my child, for this is the season of the eagle. And, you will soar like the eagle – far, far, far higher than even you could dream or imagine."

Father, I bring your precious child before you,

this child who has thought in their heart,

"My dreams are deferred, every vision comes to naught . . ."

And I release our beloved Holy Spirit's anointing to impact your weary heart today.

I release shift. Shift. Shift.

The transition into the birthing of all you have held precious under God.

And pondered in your heart.

The release of every ordained dream.

Of every one of God's promises for your life.

For your family.

For your ministry.

For your business.

For your extended household.

For your finances.

Shift, shift, shift, beloved.

One more deep breath before your promises are born.

For surely, surely, YOU WILL see God's goodness and kindness in the land of the living!

He LOVES you!

WHEN IT'S ONLY I WHO SEE . . .

*T*oday you may be facing a season in your life where it seems that even your nearest and dearest are powerless to help you.

Maybe you have been deeply let down, misunderstood, even betrayed by those you believed with all your heart would be loyal forever.

Maybe you are experiencing a season of being overlooked and unappreciated, that the immense treasure of your heart is unseen by so many.

And your weariness that even God does not see is overwhelming.

And you are tempted to value yourself based on the circumstances that presently surround you.

But, oh, dear son, dear daughter, so immensely loved by the Father.

The One who formed you with such irrepressible joy before your conception,

The One who created and marveled at all your inward parts,

Who created you to be a unique joy to Him.

Our incredible Father.

He is the One who would take you up this very day into His tender embrace and whisper gently to your heart,

"Beloved child, you are one after my heart, even as my son King David was to me.

"And I AM the One who sees."

Your Father sees every tear, every act of courage, every unseen kindness, every decision of forgiveness even on your stumbling and faltering days.

He is wooing you forward out of the wilderness and He is whispering,

"Just one more step, my beloved,

"Come, away with me . . . come . . ."
For He IS the lover of your soul
And He IS the One who sees.

IN THE NIGHT SEASON

"*I* have watched, my child, as you have endured in the night season, when there is no applause.

"When there is no man to see your work for me.

"I have watched as you have continued day after day after day, when no man saw your efforts so as to commend them and when none even knew or recognized your efforts.

"And, yes, my child, there are many, many, many of my servants who love me and minister for me, but it is those who love me and serve me when it is only I who see.

"Oh, it is to these ones that there is a great recompense of reward, for my servants are more easily encouraged with encouragement from men but it is to those who stand in the night watch that the reward will be given.

"Those who stand in the gates when there is none before them, it is to those who travail away from the public view that I would call tenderly, oh, so tenderly into my arms this day, for, my child, your effort rises up before me as a great sacrifice and your endurance, for I have been deeply touched by those who do it for me when it is only I who see.

"When it is only I who see the times when you are too tired but still you carry on.

"When it is only I who hear the breaking of your heart from the persecutions for my gospel, but still you preach my Word.

"When it is only I who see your prayers that seem to hit the ceiling yet you still choose to worship me.

"When it is only I who see your life poured out for my sake in so many, many ways that others fail to notice.

"When it is only I who see your labor in the secret place.

"When it is only I who see the kind word for a hurting soul, the patience with one unlovely.

"When it is only I who see the work never tiring into the night and 'the laying down' of that which you would prefer to do that you may please my Father.

"When it is only I who see you carry on to do my will when even you felt all your own hope was gone and yet you continued to give hope to those in need of me.

"When only I was there to see as you watched others' dreams flourish when your own were still far away.

"When only I was there to see you do so many things that did not come naturally to you but because they were essential to a furthering of my gospel.

"All these things, my child, I alone have seen.

"All these things, my child, I alone was there to see.

"And, even as when I walked the earth, so there was also a time when only my Father was there to see and even as my Father watched me, beloved, so I watch and yearn and weep for you. I watch and laugh and rejoice over you.

"So, in your darkest time, beloved, know this, when only I was there to see, I saw, I heard, and I loved . . . YOU."

Father, in the name of Jesus, beloved, I lift you before the Father today.

Those of you who deep in their hearts have cried,

"My way is unseen of the Lord."

And, Father, I ask for your beautiful presence and your glory to overshadow this one reading these very pages.

That they would know the overwhelming comfort of your Holy Spirit.

That they would sense your tangible presence. And sense your infinite mercies and know beyond any doubt that YOU are the One who sees every step they take.

That your eye is ever upon them, that their way is known by you.

That every hair on their head is numbered by you.

That they are your infinite treasure.

That YOU are the One who SEES, who loves them.

The One who will never, never leave them.

For surely you are the One who sees . . .

He LOVES you!

THE ROSE

*B*eloved friend, even in your weakest time,
Because you belong to our Lord Jesus Christ, there is more power in your little finger than in the whole of hell.

In your seeming frailty and weakness is God almighty's strength.

Even in your stumbling and your weariness, the Lord sees the mighty warrior that He created you to be.

Beautiful ones, I had a vision from the Lord and so sensed that He wanted me to share this with you.

I saw a delicate rose.

It was still attached to the stem, but the stem was bowed down and the rose itself was lying crushed on the ground.

Its petals were mostly gone and scattered all over the ground. The remains of a tiny bud remained on the stem.

Then, there was a shadow and someone was leaning over the rose bush and very, very tenderly placed the stem carefully back into place.

I knew this was Jesus, the gardener.

Jesus took out pruning shears and gently pruned the rose and the stem right down until only two-thirds of the rose was left.

Then I heard many voices of bewilderment and panic, some in despair and I knew they were the voices of those who had been through great siftings and crushing, those who had been trying desperately to pick up the crushed petals and hold the rose of their lives together themselves. Suddenly, when the Master himself cut the rose and the stem, they felt that now everything ... their hope ... their vision ... and their dreams were dead.

Oh, but then I saw that some time had passed and Jesus was walking in the garden with his Father and took him straight to the exact rose.

Oh, the wonder of that new rose. It was beautiful ... still delicate, the most pale pink, but so perfectly formed ... so healthy ... filled with the most beautiful petals. The Father Himself leaned over and smelled the rose; the fragrance of it saturated the entire garden.

And angels upon angels came to view it and looked upon it in absolute wonder!

Beloved, that rose is your future and your destiny. It is for many who have struggled through this past season of transition and wilderness. The pruning is sometimes bewildering and painful ... but, oh, what incredible days await us.

BELOVED WARRIORS

"*M*any of my children have fought with all their strength to see the proclamation of my gospel across the earth at this time.

"These are my sons and daughters who have stood and fought day after day with little encouragement, while facing so much opposition.

"These are the ones who have stood against the taunting Goliaths of this present age every day of their earthly lives.

"And even though their arms are weary, still they fight on.

"These are my beloved warriors who fight each day in the high places of the earth. I would comfort them and encourage them.

"For surely I have seen their hearts, and their innermost cries have reached up to me and have rent the heavens and quickly, quickly I am coming to them in this next season.

"They shall experience a quickening of my Spirit in their midst in a manner that they have not known before.

"For this past season has been a time of equipping. A time of preparation.

"It has been a time of standing in the hard places of the battle, but, my child, tell these ones, tell my glorious warriors that a new day of the Kingdom is dawning."

"A day of glory.

"A day of my fire and my presence.

"A day of QUICKENING in the battle.

"A day of RELEASING . . .

"For I tell you that this coming season is unlike the one that has gone before – for as many of my warriors have struggled to be resourced and equipped – I am about to release upon those that fight the battle of my kingdom a mighty outpouring of resources and equipping.

"Buildings will be released.

"Buildings and schools and even stadiums will come into the hands of my people, my steadfast warriors.

FAVOR SHALL FLOW FROM GOVERNMENTS.

"And there shall be a great releasing of favor – and favor shall flow from the governments towards these ones who proclaim my kingdom.

"Favor from kings and presidents, from prime ministers and governments. Even from Downing Street and the White House, unprecedented favor shall flow in a different flow and a different measure from what has been known before.

"And Africa and Asia shall be a part of this.

"And the voice of the Church shall begin to rise even in Europe, even in Great Britain, and this voice shall rise with CLARITY and AUTHORITY, and there shall be a shaking in the high places of Britain. But the Church shall RISE."

RELEASING OF FINANCES FOR THE WORK OF GOD.

"And there shall be a great releasing of finances for the equipping of my Church."

"From the east and the west it shall flow, from inside the Church it shall flow, but from outside the walls of the established Church, it shall start to flood, even like a torrent in this coming season."

FOR THERE HAS BEEN A WITHHOLDING FROM THE ENEMY.

"For there has been a great withholding and restraint over my ministries in this past season, but these resources belong to my warriors and to my Church. That which the devil has held, will now break the constraints of his hordes and overrun the powers of hell."

"And a great release of kingdom resources shall overtake my warriors in this coming day."

Father, my prayer for your beloved one
   Is that you would infuse your strength,
   Your power,
   Your vitality into this precious heart.
   Invigorate.
   Refresh.
   Infuse fresh hope, in the mighty, incomparable name of Jesus.
   Infuse your treasured son, your treasured daughter, with your Spirit of MIGHT.
   Strengthen them with your power in their inner man.
   Grant them not only the mighty force of faith, but grant them your HOPE.
   Oh, Father, I release a mighty impartation of your power and of fresh hope.
   Fresh hope.
   Fresh hope for the future.
   Wash away the weakness of the wilderness season and renew their clarity, renew their strength, that as your warriors, they would once again begin to mount up like the eagle.
   To once again SOAR in the upper places, basking in your glory and your presence, reinvigorated by your presence and your overwhelming love.
   Thank you for the impartation of the warrior spirit to this faithful, precious, weary soldier.

Power, power, power, power.
Might, might, might, might.
Hope, hope, hope, hope!
Amen.

YOU ARE AN OVERCOMER

*B*eloved friend, you are an overcomer. We would never need to be overcomers if there were no challenges, no battles, no fiery trials to overcome.

Oh, even in your fiery trial, in the times when the fire and the floods have threatened to overwhelm you, remember this incredible Scripture, precious one:

CONSIDER IT PURE JOY, MY BROTHERS AND SISTERS, WHENEVER YOU FACE TRIALS OF MANY KINDS, BECAUSE YOU KNOW THAT THE TESTING OF YOUR FAITH PRODUCES PERSEVERANCE. LET PERSEVERANCE FINISH ITS WORK SO THAT YOU MAY BE MATURE AND COMPLETE, NOT LACKING ANYTHING.

(James 1:2–4 NIV)

Do not be amazed when you are in the midst of fiery trials.

You are NOT abandoned, you have NOT been left desolate by the Father.

Far, far more it is because you have stood in the darkest of times, even in your weakness and frailty, even in the dark seasons of your soul, and have endured with fortitude. And courage. And persistence.

And never let go of the Father's promises to you.

Oh, my beautiful friend, I am writing words to you that have come out of the pain of walking through my own fiery trials. Trials of abandonment and trials of heartbreaking betrayals. Trials that literally press one into that secret place of crying out to the Father, Abba,

Daddy. "How could this happen?" But our Father is still weaving the tapestry of your life.

So often, we only glimpse the reverse side of it, we view the knots and the uneven stitches and cry, "I cannot see the plan." But when our incredible Father of compassion turns your tapestry over, oh, how breathtaking it will be! Every stitch will be perfectly formed. The incredible hues, the most intricately designed pattern, will be uniquely designed and planned from before your very conception in your life scroll that sits preciously and is fiercely guarded by the Father Himself.

Oh, take heart today, courageous one, for indeed it is to you, steadfast warrior, that our Father's great joy is to give you the overcomer's crown. He LOVES you!

"THE SOUND OF MY ARMY HAS BEEN HEARD IN THE KINGDOM OF DARKNESS"

"*F*or I have raised up an army that is starting to march.

"The sound of my army has been heard in the kingdom of darkness. And it has gripped their hearts with dread, for my warriors are rising – my warriors are rising.

"And there shall be a great QUICKENING – a quickening of my Holy Spirit – and a great releasing of miracles is about to pour forth from those who faithfully and steadfastly have proclaimed my kingdom.

"And I tell you that MIRACLES – miracles– yes, miracles shall flow.

A MIGHTY QUICKENING – CREATIVE MIRACLES – RISE OF WORLDWIDE PRAYER MOVEMENT

"And there shall be a mighty quickening and creative miracles shall be released in a manner never before seen across the earth – for there shall be a quickening of my Spirit."

"And there shall be a quickening of prayer and prayer movements shall start to rise across the face of the earth.

"This shall not be man-made but it shall be of me.

"They shall rise in Asia, they shall rise in Africa, they shall rise in the United Kingdom, they shall rise across America, they shall rise in Europe and across the Middle East; they shall rise as one, in a short season of time.

"A worldwide prayer movement shall rise. It shall appear as an organized prayer movement, but it will be organized by no man, but by my Spirit says the Lord. I and the Father are one."

Father, I lift up your warriors today and I release in the mighty name of Jesus brand-new strength, fresh encouragement.

Reinvigorate them with YOUR purpose, mighty Father,

to accomplish great and mighty works for you, to be executors of your purposes and plans on Earth in this new season.

Oh, Father, I release fresh courage. fresh hope.

Fresh strength to continue. Oh, Father grant them the visionary eyesight of the eagle that they might see beyond the veil, beyond the raging storms, beyond the disappointments, as you reach out your strong right arm and whisper, "Take my hand, Oh, beloved of my heart, and come. Come walk with me into new joy and freedom, into everything planned and purposed for you." Release. Release.

Release from Heaven to Earth every mantle, every tool, everything you have need of. For you are His exceeding JOY!

YOU WERE BORN FOR SUCH A DAY

*B*eloved one, you were born into the earth for such a day, for such a time, for such a generation as this.

Your Father chose the exact hour, day and time of your birth.

He knew the challenges you would encounter on the way, but far more than that, He knew that you were born to the battle and that you were born for the battle, so He placed a core of Himself in the very depths of your being. A core of His strength. A core of His courage.

A core of His endurance and fortitude, for you were chosen to be His WARRIOR.

So often, we lose sight of the fact, as followers of Jesus, the persecutions and the trials that his disciples faced. As the Church today, we are taught victory alone, and of course . . . victory in him is our exceeding and ultimate goal. But when we take a look at the soldiers of past earthly wars, the carnage on the beaches of Dunkirk that was so movingly displayed in the movie "Saving Private Ryan" it was horrific. So often we forget that before every great victory there is a great battle. A battle against our perfectly tidy worlds (that we long for in our natural minds) to keep safe and secure and tidy at all costs. But we have had a clarion call . . . a call to arms from Heaven itself, our Savior's question, "Will you fight in my army?"

"Onward Christian soldiers, marching as to war,

with the cross of Jesus going on before . . ." Jesus never demands that we enroll but still he gently asks the question, "Will you pick up your cross and follow me?" It is a hard saying. Such a hard saying, beloved.

I have reached the point many times where I cried out to the Lord,

"It is too hard, Lord Jesus, how much MORE of my life do you require?

"I am stumbling already, I am filled, filled, with such humanity and frailties." And I hear His, oh, so tender voice, "Can you follow me?

Can you give up your safe, tidy world? I do not demand it, but I cannot use you to the fullest if you choose to stay on the home front. Can you follow me into the heat of battle for souls? Can you follow me, beloved warrior, and pay the price of a soldier?"

Oh, Lord Jesus, our hearts want to, but our flesh makes us weak.

Strengthen us in your mercy, we pray, to carry the banner of your glorious name, to reach the lost and dying. Beloved friend, you are SO incredible. The road that many of you have chosen has been this very road. Oh, how Jesus loves you. Oh, how proud he is of you. Truly YOU are his treasure.

Father, in the glorious name of Jesus, I ask that today you would release the spirit of MIGHT into your weary warrior. The spirit of MIGHT and WISDOM.

Strengthen their weary arms, make straight the crooked paths, and set them on a high place that they may see the battlefield like an eagle.

Grant them discernment to know when to fight and when to be still.

Wisdom to discern the times and the seasons, renewed ability to hear your still, small voice, and courage to obey.

O, beloved Father, bless them. Bless them. Bless them this day.

Reward their faithfulness, merciful Father, grant them their hearts' desires.

Let them taste your GOODNESS in the land of the living. Let joy and peace and renewed hope be their portion. Forever and ever,

Amen.

NEW LIFE –
WAR AND WORSHIP

"*A*nd I have equipped you with my Holy Spirit and with my FIRE," says the Lord of Hosts.

"And even as you have been trained up in the hard places and the wilderness of testing of faith and endurance,

"Of storms and challenges and persecutions,

"These things that have been your foes in the past shall become your meat and your weaponry to fight in this coming season.

"I am calling my warriors to war and to worship, for I have developed in you my endurance and I have grown fortitude in you and the strength of my kings of old.

"And even as David fought with one hand and worshipped with the other, so too I am raising up in this day and in this hour – WARRIORS, WARRIORS, WARRIORS all across the earth – from the North and the South – from the East and the West – warriors who will war with one hand and worship with the other.

"For I am calling my warriors in this last Church age to war and to worship.

"I am calling all who I birthed for the battle to war and to worship for the strength to endure and to persevere.

"And to wage a mighty death blow to the enemy which shall come from your worship in the SECRET PLACE, in the cleft of the rock.

"For it is there that even as I poured out my strategies to my servant David, that I shall pour out my strategies unto you.

"The fire of my presence shall fall.

"So seek my face, my warrior, seek my face.

"Call upon my name.

"Draw into my presence.

"And the fire of my presence shall fall and consume, the FIRE of my presence shall fall and consume, and you shall be girded with strength for the battle.

"And you shall be girded with power and with might and with divine strategy to prevail against the gates of hell.

"Lift up your weary arms, my son, my daughter, make straight the crooked paths, for you were BORN to the battle – you were BORN to war."

YOU ARE A DREAMER

*O*h, don't give up now, dear friend. I know one amazing woman who was divorced after twenty-seven years and God brought her the most amazing husband. They have been so happily married for twelve years. Another beautiful story. I cannot mention this minister's name but you would know her! She was so desperately lonely after her divorce.

She was literally crying out to God in the shower, "Father, I cannot be alone anymore." And then she met and married a minister.

And together they heralded in one of the greatest renewal revivals ever seen in the past two decades. Gwen Shaw from End Time Handmaidens was divorced after twenty-eight years, and the Lord brought her beloved 'General' to her, and they ministered together for over thirty years until they both went to Heaven. So today I so sense the Father is saying,

"Take heart, O desperately lonely one. Yes, there are those I have called out to me but I said it was not good that man should be alone.

"Your case is before me and I will not let you down! You are IN PROCESS! I have no intention of leaving you like this.

"So take my hand, just a few more steps, A bit more patience, and more healing of your abandoned heart." Oh He loves you!

He loves you! He loves you! He will not leave you comfortless.

PROPHECY:

Oh, the Father would say to you today, "Oh, my beloved dreamer, dust off the disappointments of yesterday, of yesteryear.

"Dust off the weariness, the loss of faith in the dreams that I placed so long ago deep in your heart. For, yes, it is true that hope deferred made many of you heartsick and you carefully rewrapped your dreams and replaced them deep inside your heart but I tell you, my beloved son, beloved daughter, today is a NEW day and I am wooing you back to once again be my dreamer."

"And in the same manner as Abraham and Daniel and Joseph before you, I am reaching my hand out to you and declaring, it is TIME for YOUR DREAM."

"And yet you say, 'O Father, it has been too hard. I am weary. I have ploughed on hard soil.'

So the Father says, "And yes, even as those who went before you, this is true.

"But, child, there was a sovereignly appointed day,

"A sovereignly appointed hour, when Heaven watching cried,

"'It is time for the dream.' Your life scroll lies before me

"And the dreams that I birthed in you for this earth, for you to achieve for me, are written in the very days of your life,

"The dreams that are unique only to you,

"The dreams that you were given your very breath to create,

"For the enemy's purpose in the valley of the shadow and the fiery wilderness were to weaken your faith,

"To tarnish the very dreams that signify your purpose.

"But, beloved, I reach out to you today to call out the dreamer inside you, to dust off the weariness of yesterday, to infuse fresh hope, fresh vision, fresh joy inside your heart. So take my hand, beloved dreamer, take my hand and know that I am still the God of the impossible.

"I AM the God who makes ALL things NEW. I am the incubator of your dreams, for your dreams are my dreams.

"And even as my servant Joseph languished in the pit and in the prison, even as my servant Joseph grieved in the late night hour,

'Where is this dream that I dreamed that was so tangible when I was young?' In JUST ONE DAY, in just one day, I took my servant Joseph from behind the bars of his prison and elevated him to be the second in command of Egypt!

"One day, beloved, CHANGES EVERYTHING. One day, and the impossible became possible. One day and the insurmountable became achievable.

"One day and every dream for years and years came into technicolor reality. So, dust off your dreams this day, beloved. And KNOW that as you speak, I speak and know that as you renew your faith, the power and might and resurrection power of I AM is backing you.

"Oh, take my hand beloved dreamer . . .

". . . for it is time for YOUR Dream!"

SEASON OF LONELINESS

"*B*eloved child of my heart,

I have watched as you have wrestled in anguish as the loneliness of your soul has threatened to overwhelm you like a fierce tide washing over your soul, threatening to drown out your faith and your hope for the future.

"For it has been in this season of warfare and in this season of stripping of many things near and dear from you that where once you were totally secure in all that was temporal around you, you turned around to find that many, many of the earthly comforts that you had walked with for years were now nowhere in sight.

"And I heard your cry, 'Why?'

"Yes, I heard your cry, 'Why, Father?'

"Yes, I have seen every tear of anguish that you have shed and my heart has broken with your own heart for, my child, I am the God who sees. I am the God who understands your frame and knows that you are dust.

"And, as my great compassions rise up to meet you in this hour, open your heart to me, beloved child, for there was One who was lonely before you.

"For child, beloved child, my creation, my beloved creation, abandoned me. And the loneliness I feel, as I yearn for fellowship with those of my children who are separated from me in this present day and in this hour, this is the very reason that I sent my Son, that I may be reconciled to those whom I love.

"Oh, beloved, how my own heart has yearned for you in the midnight hour as you have broken with the grief and the excruciating emotion of loneliness. But, even as I rejoice and my heart is healed with each soul that returns to me, do you think that I would leave you in your present state?

"No! Oh, no!

"Beloved son, beloved daughter of my heart, your heart is ever before me.

"And, as I tenderly remove your life scroll and place it before me, I tell you that every day, yes every day of your life has been written. You have not been left forsaken.

"And, even as my servant Job received restitution and restoration of all things, so too, my child, restoration and great and joyful restitution is yours.

"For as your cry has risen up to me, so too in my courts of Heaven a great cry has gone forth: 'JUSTICE and judgments will be ruled against the enemy on your behalf.'

"So, beloved, take fresh hope this day, take fresh hope this very day, knowing that I am your great Deliverer.

"Know that I, the Lord God of Israel, am your Restorer. Know that not only will I bind up your broken heart, that I will heal your wounds and bind up the broken places, but that your redemption draws nigh.

"And when you see that day, beloved, know this, that it was I, the Lord, your Emperor and your King, who through my great and tender compassions for you, rained down joy and love and my goodness upon your life.

"And in the land of the living you will still see my goodness.

"In the land of the living you will still see my great hand of mercy.

"For my love for you is unsearchable.

"My love for you is inextinguishable.

"My love for you is eternal."

THE FATHER'S LOVE

*O*h, how the Father loves you.

Oh, how the Father loves you.

Oh, how beautiful you are to Him.

Oh, how He yearns for you, that you would run to Him as a little child and climb onto His lap.

Oh, how He would sing over you with His love.

Oh, how He yearns to talk with you.

For, He yearned for you so much, that He could not live in eternity without you.

So, He sent His only beloved Son to die for you, that YOU, His most beautiful treasure, would be reconciled back to His heart in intimate fellowship with Him.

Oh, how Jesus loves you.

Oh, how the Holy Spirit loves you.

And, how our most beautiful Father loves you.

You are all beautiful to Him.

In you He finds no flaw.

He knows every weakness, each besetting sin, but still He adores you.

You are His beautiful child,

You are HIS!!!

THE FAIRY TALE

A PROPHETIC WORD

*M*y beautiful friends,
I felt the Lord saying:

"Your fairy tale is being written in Heaven right at this moment."

I see a mighty release of scribe ANGELS picking up your life scrolls and the Father says, "ACCELERATION . . . acceleration." The scribe angels are opening your life scrolls and writing.

I see these same scrolls then being handed to angels on assignment who are ministering on your behalf and being commissioned all across the earth to move circumstances, challenges, and practical obstacles – out of the PATH of the DESTINY of your life!

Oh, the Father's word today is:

"FAIRY TALE . . . fairy tale.

"My beloved Child,

"I am the creator of dreams . . .

"I am the great story teller . . .

"And this day I am accelerating angelic intervention to start to bring about all those events written in your life scroll of DESTINY!"

I see the words, 'DIVINE ALIGNMENT.'

And I see scales that have been weighted out of sync. The Father is adjusting the scales of your life this very day into divine alignment.

I see the words:

RESTITUTION.

RESTORATION.

BROKEN PLACES MENDED.

A great release of suddenly.

HEALINGS that have been held back by the enemy.

I see FINANCES, CONTRACTS, HOUSES being released to you.

I see the most incredible wave.

It is huge, like a Tsunami of held-back blessings, and it is right now being released from the throne room of the Father.

Oh! Jesus, the Father and the Holy Spirit are having such incredible JOY over this!

A defeat after, in some instances many months, even years, of held-back blessings pouring right towards you and over you from the portals of Heaven. From the very hand of the Father.

"Release! Release! Release!"

Is Heaven's cry.

Where you have felt constrained, confused and in such a very narrow place, the Father has decreed:

"The walls are coming down!

"I am writing fairy tales. Fairy tales today . . . rejoice, rejoice, beloved, beloved child:

"FOR YOU ARE MINE!"

THE BIRTHDAY PARTY DRESS

Beloved darling hearts,

This is for all of you. So very many have messaged me about how broken their hearts are. This is from my personal experience in Heaven with Jesus and the Father.

I found myself in the Father's garden.

I was about four or five years old, dressed in the most amazing birthday party dress.

I was holding balloons in my hand.

And presents.

So, so excited to go to the party and as I looked up at the Father,

I was full of innocence and child-like trust in joyful anticipation of all that awaited me.

The Father looked upon me (as He does you) with such joy and pride.

And then I ran off in eager anticipation.

What seemed hours later I returned, running to the Father.

But now my exquisite birthday party dress was torn and muddied, And full of briers.

I was sobbing.

And my balloons were still in my hand, but they were all deflated.

I flung myself into the Father's arms.

And I cried,

"Daddy . . . Daddy . . . Abba . . ."

And I could not talk, for the absolute devastation and pain that was in my heart.

I had gone to the party in such child-like trust and anticipation,

And my little heart had been rejected.

And I was completely confused and bewildered.

The Father gathered me up in His arms and held me, oh, so tightly to His chest and rocked me and rocked me until my sobbing eventually stopped.

I looked up at the Father through my tears.

"Daddy . . . I was hurt . . . so badly."

The Father, oh, so gently took my face in His hands.

"Beloved, princess . . . my princess,

"People who are wounded . . . wound others.

"It is not rejection of you, it seems so very personal but it is as a result of their own wounds that they have carried, oftentimes for decades.

"And if those wounds are not dealt with and healed and delivered, they can and will be triggered in the most unexpected of circumstances.

"Although it seems SO extremely personal, beloved child, it is nothing to do with you or your beautiful, open heart.

"Tell my beloved sons and daughters that many, many of the seeming rejections they have encountered have been because of unhealed wounding in their wives and husbands . . . in their relationships.

"But," and the Father was very fierce in this,

"I am about to sweep these ones with healing and deliverance.

"With sovereign and divine encounters.

"I am about to bring things that have even been hidden for decades into my light.

"The gatekeepers that have held them captive will now be exposed, and I will HEAL them."

And many of you are saying, 'Surely it is too far gone?'"

But the Father says,

"Watch and see my right hand move in power and in might and in mercy, and you will see my hand restore in the Land of the Living . . ."

A WALK WITH JESUS
IN HIS GARDEN

Beautiful, beloved warriors,

So many of us are feeling that a major shift is about to occur in the spirit realm. Many of us are already strongly sensing the change that is about to break upon us.

And then my heart got a direct hit. A very personal situation that affected me deeply was trying to knock me back in the most vulnerable place. I felt I had no emotional reserves left to stand against the attack. I was too weary.

And then I heard Jesus say , "My beloved child, my precious daughter, "Come walk in my garden . . .

"What I share with you I want you to share with my beautiful sons and daughters, for many are experiencing a similar setback as you all move forward out of transition."

I said, "Daddy, my heart is so sore I don't even have the strength to come."

But I knew Jesus was waiting for me.

I closed my eyes and I was suddenly in the vast meadow, lying in a bed of crocuses under a huge, very tall old tree.

I lay with my face in the bed of flowers, literally unable to find the reserves to move my head.

How long I lay there I don't know, except that the pain in my heart wouldn't stop.

And it seemed nothing I did could take it away.

There were some small animals that darted past, but I still couldn't lift my head.

Then I sensed activity around me and I knew it was angelic.

And I was gently turned around as some kind of liniment was tenderly rubbed on my chest.

And my feet were being washed with immense tenderness.

I asked what the angels were using to wash my feet.

"We are anointing your feet on the instruction of the Father so that you will have the strength to walk the final short stretch of His yellow brick road, where RESTORATION AND RESTITUTION awaits you. You have gone as far as you can."

Then Jesus was suddenly beside me.

Oh, he looked down upon me so tenderly, with such mercy and understanding.

"The immense and brutal attack that you experienced yesterday was strategically intended to knock you off your feet and weaken your heart and soul so that you were robbed of the strength to walk the final steps OUT OF TRANSITION.

"Many of my children have been experiencing cruel attacks against their heart and emotions as they near the finish line.

"We in Heaven know this, and our angels have been released with vials of strength and vigor and deep balm for my children's hearts and emotions in these past few days."

He was very gentle.

"Know this, beloved son, beloved daughter, the cruel and targeted attack of the enemy that was meant to break your heart was meant to be as a magnitude-10 earthquake.

"Tell my children that I am now scaling down the vicious attack of the enemy to a magnitude of 1 on your Richter scale.

"You yourself will not even understand why, when it should have destroyed your heart and emotions.

"You will walk through it virtually unscathed and in the weeks and months you shall see such a glorious turnaround in this circumstance.

"And this DECREE is not only for you. It is for many, many of my sons and daughters who are experiencing the same things.

"So lift you weary head, my child and strengthen your feeble knees."

And, as I lifted my head, I saw a signpost that read HOPE.

"I am placing a divine, golden shield in this day over my children's hearts and emotions as they walk through to their FINAL FREEDOM.

"To where the enemy thought: 'He . . . she is done. Direct hit. Out for the count'.

"He has overplayed his hand."

"Oh, Jesus," I said.

"So many of us have walked through so, so much but had courage and stood and stood . . ."

Jesus was quiet.

Then he answered:

"You are all on the very last bend of the road. The enemy has just fired his last assault with ferocious intent to knock many of my children off their course. But he has lost, and real victory is in sight.

"My Father's GOODNESS in THE LAND OF THE LIVING is now within your grasp.

"Practical tokens of our love and provision on every side are about to be released from Heaven in such MAGNITUDE that the evil one will run, cowering from the tsunami of my goodness that is about to be poured out upon my faithful children who have stood in this past season.

"My Promises.

"My Provision.

"My Joy.

"My restitution for everything stolen.

"Restoration of companionship.

"Relationships.

"Finances.

"Businesses exploding.

"Global ministries being birthed.

"Powerful marketplace ministries being birthed."

"Prodigals returning home.

"And I will pour a great blessing upon those who have cried out in loneliness.

"I am releasing romantic relationships.

"I am releasing Boazes for my Ruths. And Ruths for my Boazes.

"Books will be written.

"Many new worship songs will be sung.

"Many of my servants will move out of transition, straight into an ACCELERATED DAY OF WONDERS,

"Where they shall release my GLORY and my PRESENCE across the earth in a magnitude previously unseen."

I was sitting up by now.

I frowned at Jesus.

"My heart still hurts, Jesus."

And then, my beloved, beloved, beautiful hearts,

Jesus picked me up, flung me around in his arms, looking deeply into my eyes and laughing with abandon.

"Not for long!

"I told you. You and many others will see the TURNAROUND."

And Jesus was dancing with such joy.

"Just a few more steps, beloved ones," he said.

Then he smiled broadly,

And was gone . . .

Let's all stand together my beloved, beloved warriors, as we enter the final steps to all that he has promised us.

As a family we march forward. Our eyes are fixed on our beautiful King, the Lover of our souls.

Jesus, we love you so much!

THE JIGSAW PUZZLE

A PROPHETIC WORD

Dearest ones,

The Lord showed me a vision where someone was sitting over a large jigsaw puzzle that had once been a complete picture.

It had fallen to the ground and was now in hundreds of pieces.

They were trying desperately to rebuild it in exactly the same format as it used to be.

But they were becoming more and more distressed and frustrated because so many of the pieces seemed to be missing and there were huge gaps and holes which previously had been filled to create this beautiful picture.

No matter how long they tried, they simply could NOT make the pieces fit.

Then Jesus, oh, so gently, took the pieces out of their hands, and lifted their faces to his.

"The old has gone," he said gently.

"The old has passed away. Let it go, beloved."

And, again, oh, so tenderly he removed the last piece of the puzzle from the person's hand.

In his hands was now the most beautiful-looking box.

It was tied with an exquisite ribbon.

Jesus handed it to the one sitting in despair and frustration on the floor.

"Open it," he said softly.

The person opened it quietly, still in despair.

Inside was another jigsaw puzzle.

But, oh, this one was so beautiful.

So exquisite.

Jesus nodded.

And the person began to build it.

Every single piece swiftly and easily went into perfect formation.

Until the most exquisite picture emerged.

Not a gap in sight.

Jesus smiled.

"You have been trying so desperately in your own strength and with all your might to put back the pieces of your last season.

"Crying in despair . . . because no matter how hard you tried, nothing worked as it did before.

"But you see, beloved child . . .

"It is a new season . . .

"A new wineskin in your life.

"I cannot allow you to build the new with any of the old.

"What seems so safe and familiar to you, that which you are desperately grasping for, is no longer within your reach.

"Because I have sovereignly moved you forward into the beginnings of a NEW DAY.

"Do not look back to the past.

"For I am placing my future in your hands.

"Perfectly formed;

"Perfectly fitting;

"In my rest;

"Not one piece missing.

"Not a rescaled upgrade of the old.

"But a BRAND-NEW season.

"Filled with restoration.

"Restitution.

"Joy and laughter.

"Peace that remains.

"Rest that is eternal."

And I saw the words

"For I have given you HOPE and a FUTURE"

"And no longer will you say, 'Where, where is my God?'

"But you will see Him in His glory.

"In His fullness.

"In His great compassion.

"As the rebuilder of dreams that seemed deferred and hope that became hopeless.

"And the sound of JOY and GREAT REJOICING shall once again be heard and resound within your walls.

"Justice! Justice! Justice!" cries the Lord.

"Great recompense of reward, for I AM the Lord your GOD who sees, I am your great Redeemer. REDEEMER.

"Watch the physical boundaries of your life now fall into good places for I AM with you," says the Lord.

"And I have raised my mighty hand from Heaven and declared YOUR NEW DAY!"

SATAN'S TROPHY ROOM

SEER VISION

The Father showed me incredible things. The first was a huge crystal dome. It was called, HOPE DEFERRED.

Inside the dome was a huge, most incredible array of crystal glittering lights. The dome was filled with a wondrous, almost fairy-tale glow.

It was filled with wonder.

I said, "Father, what are the fairy lights?"

He said, "Each glowing light is a promise to my precious sons and daughters that have been delayed or hijacked by the enemy.

These are my promises of my goodness, my kindness, and my overwhelming faithfulness in the land of the living."

I said, "Daddy, but why are they here?"

"Because, my beloved child in these past few years the major strategies of the enemy have been to contend so violently for my children's hope, to try to literally hijack and delay the fulfilment of my promises on earth, so that so many, many of my children have become heartsick because of so many of their dreams and hope being deferred."

I said, "O Father, how do we get it back?"

Oh, beloved, it was the most beautiful dome I had ever seen . . . there was peace and joy and wonder and new life bursting inside that dome.

"First, let me show you something," said the Father.

I looked and saw an enormous glass vat; it reached to the ceiling and was filled with rainbows and a see-through liquid like water.

The Father spoke again, "This vat is filled with my children's tears. They are tears of JOY."

"Oh, Daddy," I gasped.

"They are the tears of joy that have been stolen and delayed because the promises have been so delayed in this past season."

The Father was so anguished.

"The enemy saw that much ground was being taken and so in this past season his strategy became more violent against my champions.

"He knew that those who have loved and served me so faithfully would never, never, give up so he strategically contended for every promise and to circumvent the fulfillment of my promises and to delay and hijack my promises of goodness in the land of the living.

"Many, many, so many of my children were used to miracles manifesting in their lives, but these same champions in the past few years have been crying out to me, saying, 'Father, I have stood, I have been faithful but what used to so easily manifest, the miracles that would come overnight ... there is just barrenness and continual contending and fighting in the Spirit for what never seems to manifest.'"

The Father said, "Beloved, beloved of my heart ... this was a targeted strategy of the enemy; he could not keep the answers from you forever, but in this past season in the spirit realm, the powers and principalities have been contending violently for every promise, for they knew that this would wear down my saints." My eyes started to be drawn to a third dome. It was once again full of wonder but each time I was drawn to it a huge eruption of sheer joy would come from my heart.

"Oh, Father, he has stolen our joy."

"That, my child, is the JOY of my promises fulfilled on earth. My promises and my miracles. My kindness and my goodness in the Land of the Living. For the ultimate strategy of the enemy was to erode my children's strength."

"Because your joy is our strength," I murmured.

I sighed "But, Daddy, we are meant to have that anyhow just by being with you." Oh, the Father is so wonderful I could sense Him laughing at me. We had had certain conversations earlier today.

"Yes, my beloved princess. That you know is true . . ."

Oh, He was still laughing. "But as your Father, your Daddy, the Lover of your soul, I understand that you live on the earth and that so many times you see through a glass darkly and hold on to me by faith, so it is my utmost JOY to answer your cries for promises and my miracles. Oh, what joy it gives me when I see your tears of joy and your wonder;

"For I AM GOODNESS. I AM KINDNESS. I AM COMPASSION.

"And I yearn to see my children thriving and joyous. I love giving my children good things. I watch them even as you watched your own children open their presents and took such joy in their joy.

"I am your Father. I take such joy in your joy."

"So, Daddy, how do we get this back . . . ?"

"Remember Daniel? When Gabriel called on Michael, there was a twenty-one-day delay. As my children release the hosts of Heaven in this season, you will see as restitution of these three things that I have shown you, for it is time to demand them back in the spirit realm.

"For I tell you that ENOUGH IS ENOUGH. The time of transition is upon you. The last snares are being broken, and the victory is assured.

"And miracles are about to BREAK FORTH in the Land of the Living.

"A NEW DAY AND A NEW SEASON. Different from what has gone before.

"I told you I would break through for you so that others may have HOPE."

I said, "Daddy, you mean the three-year battle with my book rights?"

"Yes, beloved child. The battle was fierce. There were many days it seemed impossible, but they are back in your hands just as I promised they would be."

"Oh yes, Daddy, it was such a miracle."

"And you signed your contract with HarperCollins?"

"Oh, yes, Daddy." I said. "The rights came back just in time, one day later and it would have been too late, two incredible breakthroughs after three years . . ." I could feel the Father smile.

"And so now for my children, when this battle is over, miracles after miracles will break forth and the sounds of wonder and laughter and tears of joy will be my children's heritage, so pray, beloved ones, pray."

"Release the hosts of Heaven to tear down these STRONGHOLDS in the enemy's camp for even as for Daniel, your answers are on their way.

"Joy,

"Peace,

"Hope,

"Renewed wonder,

"Promises fulfilled,

"Delays finished and aborted situations resurrected,

"A new day,

"A new season,

"New strength,

"New vigor,

"New focus,

"FOR I AM THE I AM,

"The restorer of the breach,

"The binder of the broken hearted."

"Your compassionate, loving King of all kings.

"I am the Lover of your soul.

"Oh, how I yearn for you, beloved."

Your Abba, your King.

THE LAST PUSH –
FLYING BY INSTRUMENTS

Darling hearts,

The Father brought to my spirit that when an aircraft hits a storm, the pilot's normal instinctive response becomes untrustworthy.

His 'natural' reaction would cause him to make inaccurate and inappropriate responses and crash, because he is, at this moment, flying completely blind.

The intense and overriding response he has is to fly by his instincts.

But, his instincts, no matter how well trained he is, will be incorrect.

He has only one option that will save his life and the life of his passengers, and that is to disregard all the information that his natural senses are telling him and only trust flying by the plane's instruments.

We are so often the same.

When a devastating storm hits our lives and our circumstances, every sense we have is screaming, "React, react!"

But, beloved friend, we only have one course that will bring us absolute surety and enable us to land safely when everything else is screaming havoc and that is to fly by our instruments:

God's Word and His PROMISES to us.

That is called STANDING.

So STAND.

I know that for many of you, it seems that all hell has broken loose.

But the Father would say to you today,

"Hold steady, my child, my beloved child. Hold steady and hold your course.

"Do not deviate to the left or to the right.

"When all your senses are screaming, 'This is the wrong course,' hold steady.

"The enemy has put up a smokescreen and it cannot be trusted.

"It's at this time when your mind, will and emotions are at their most vulnerable, that your senses cannot be trusted.

"Speak my Word, beloved child.

"Decree my Word over your storm; decree my Word over the smokescreen.

"Fly by my instruments and you will see the storm start to clear, for I have a safe landing place for you.

"When everything within you is screaming, 'Father, all hell is breaking loose,' know this, that my ministering spirits assigned to you are clearing your path to victory and to safety.

"Hold steady, beloved one.

"Hold steady, and you will see, as the storm subsides, as the smokescreen dissolves,

"You will see the landing place that I have prepared for you.

"Green pastures,

"Refreshing,

"And rest for your weary soul.

"An oasis of pure, fresh living water.

"Dreams finally fulfilled and my promises to you fulfilled.

"Hold steady during the storm, beloved. Do not be swayed to the left or to the right, for I AM the I AM,

"And it is I who have made a path through the storm for you.

"Take a deep breath, beloved child.

"You are SO near to your breakthrough.

"Just put your hand in mine

"And fly by the instruments.

"My Word,

"The counsel of my Holy Spirit,

"My unwavering promises.

"The turbulence of these past few years is almost at an end.

"Your safe haven is now in sight.

"Hold on just a bit longer,

"And STAND.

"For I have not only provided the safe place for you to land;

"It is your place called THERE,

"An OPEN-HEAVEN.

"Breakthrough at last.

"ALL PROVISION.

"Oh, how you will rejoice.

"So, place your weary hand in mine, beloved of my heart,

"And STAND.

"Knowing ALL THINGS will be WELL.

"All will be well.

"The storm and turbulence of your life are about to be transformed into the greatest blessing that will impact EVERY area of your life.

"Take heart,

"O courageous one.

"Take heart,

"For I, the I AM,

"The anchor of your soul, I am with you."

Thank you, Father!
Oh, grant us the grace this day to fly by your instruments and stand,
As we fly towards your place called THERE.
From my heart to your heart always.

JOSEPH

*N*one of us, until we reach Heaven, can fully know or understand the seasons Joseph must have gone through.

Imagine, he was promised that his gift of dream interpretation would be remembered and mentioned before Pharaoh, but then that promise was forgotten.

He had to continue on with no idea how long he would stay confined in captivity.

This was already after he had been thrown into the pit by his brothers.

His multicolored coat was a gift from his father, signifying the incredible and huge destiny on his life – his God-given and ordained mantle.

Many of us find ourselves in similar situations, presently standing on, or clinging on, what feels like our last breath.

We're walking, one foot in front of the other, each day wondering: "Is this the day? Is this the day of release when all of God's promises and suddenlies will manifest ?"

Then, waking up in the morning and once again, the captivity is still there. So we cry out to God for His infinite grace.

We cry out to the Father for more courage and for more strength to face (and continue walking through) those things in our lives.

Things in the natural are threatening to crush our souls, yet, we walk one more step and take one more deep breath.

But today, oh such beloved hearts, I hear the Father saying: "I have heard your cries.

"Oh beloved, beloved struggling one, your cries have reached my altar. They have rent the heavens and as I look down upon your weary heart, Heaven is filled with uproarious joy.

"Dust off the multicolored mantle I have given you.

For even as Joseph's suddenly manifested, your destiny, your journey of such incredible faith and fortitude is ever before me.

And your determination – even in the days of greatest weakness – rises up before my throne as a beautiful fragrance as it was with Cornelius.

"... AND SAID, 'CORNELIUS, GOD HAS HEARD YOUR PRAYER AND REMEMBERED YOUR GIFTS TO THE POOR' "
(Acts 10:31 KJV)

"Even as with Cornelius's alms (gifts), I am always, always in remembrance of you.

"And, yes, I have heard your cry, 'How long, God? How long? It seems the prison walls are closing in on me.'

"And here is my promise to you today, oh weary, beloved one: God's promises and suddenlies will manifest!

"If Joseph had been released from prison in his time, the time he asked to be remembered before Pharaoh, he would have been released.

But released as an ORDINARY MAN ... and gone about his business.

Let me say that again ... oh, beloved ... this is such a profound truth ...

Joseph would either have stagnated in captivity or been released – not as second in charge to Pharaoh, ruler over Egypt, but released back into life as an ordinary man but I, the I AM, the One who ordained him, who called him, who appointed him unto a great and incredible destiny – had to ensure that he was passed over and seemingly forgotten or else his destiny would have been aborted.

"And so, he continued day by day overlooked – seemingly passed over.

Such hope that had arisen in his heart was deferred, left to the day-to-day still in captivity, living with unfulfilled destiny in his heart and the passion of my promises burning in his bones. Your "Pharaoh" and destiny will intersect. For I had every day of Joseph's life written in his life-scroll. And I knew the exact day, the precise hour, the exact moment, when destiny would converge with circumstances.

"So I had to ensure that while Joseph cried out to me, 'Your promise, Father . . . release me!' – that it was in that holy vortex where Joseph's destiny and his apostolic mantle to deliver Egypt – would intersect.

Therefore he seemed forgotten, for I knew there was another day.

For I knew there was another day marked in Heaven. A day marked in destiny when Pharaoh's heart was ready to be moved. And so, Joseph came before Pharaoh and he was appointed as second in command to Pharaoh – the deliverer of Egypt.

"And so it is with so many of you, beloved.

Your suddenly awaits you – your heavenly intersection of timing.

Your 'Pharaoh' and destiny will suddenly intersect and oh, what rejoicing you will have!

"Oh, hold on beloved. Hold on beloved. Hold on to me.

"For your suddenly time of destiny will not evade you.

It is on its way.

It is coming.

It is coming and all of Heaven rejoices – rejoices.

And I will do things in a day that you have waited for years to manifest.

And you shall lift up your head and your eyes to me, the great Lover of your soul."

Love, Your *Abba* Father.

SEER ENCOUNTER FROM THE FATHER

LAY DOWN YOUR BROOM CINDERELLA – YOU ARE GOING TO THE BALL!

*T*he Father says, "I'm calling my Cinderella." Beautiful hearts, this is one of the most important seer encounters I have ever experienced.

I was awakened at 6.00 am this morning. I said to the Father, "Oh, Abba, Daddy, I need to go to your garden." I was very small, like a toddler sitting on my Father's lap . . . clinging to Him and suddenly He said, "Cinderella, you are going to the ball!"

I said religiously, "Oh, Father, Cinderella's not in the Bible."

And I could sense His joy and He said, "My beloved Son used to tell parables. This is my parable. My Cinderellas today. Cinderellas are all of my sons and daughters who have felt isolated.

Their dreams have become faded memories. My beloved Cinderellas have been living in survival mode for so long, living day to day in the wilderness, in seeming barrenness, using the last of their courage to survive the day, put to hard task by the enemy of their souls."

Then the Father said.

"For so many of my children who have been through divorce and such adverse circumstances it has been a long season of being a Cinderella under the cruel and ruthless hardship driven by the cruel stepsisters. The enemy has in this past season reduced so many of my most precious children to walking in the rags of lost hope, their dreams deferred . . . that my Cinderellas can hardly even believe that there is a BALL."

Tell my sons, tell my daughters, that this day . . . this very day, I am releasing from Heaven itself the cry, 'Beloved Cinderella, precious child of my heart, you are about to be released from your long, hard servitude in the wilderness . . . for I am calling to you from Heaven, from my throne room. Cinderella, you are going to the Ball. My Cinderellas have been watching others going to the ball for so long in this season, that many, many have completely given up thinking that they would ever go to the ball themselves . . . but the fairy-tale carriage is there. It awaits them, and I am about to exchange their rags and work clothes for the most incredible ball gown they have ever seen, and I am escorting them with my angelic host. The exchange of their past season of isolation. Of hardship. Of aridness. Of survival mode . . . .and exchange the rags for beauty. Lay down your broom, Cinderella, the enemy has been raging against you for too long . . . he has been cruel and ruthless against you . . . even as the stepsisters were to Cinderella, knowing, sensing the destiny upon her life. Lay down your broom that signifies the past season of hardship and survival and look before you for I have laid out your ball gown and your sparkling dancing shoes. Wash your face from the tears, for you are my Esther, my Deborah, my princess . . .

The King has called for you . . .

Cinderella, you are going to the ball!"

I looked down at myself and I was dressed in rags, my hands were work-worn, no make-up, living in survival mode so, so long, just having the courage for the day . . .

And the Father said, "Enough is enough, my princesses, you are going to the ball . . . and nothing and no enemy can stop their destiny which is about to come forth." And I watched and saw that the Father's

Cinderellas had been so beaten down, were so, so weary, had lost sight of their dreams that once lived in vibrant technicolor that they couldn't even believe that they would actually ever get to the ball . . .

Then the Father said. "The carriage is waiting . . . your ball gown is laid out . . . the winds of change are blowing . . . your tide is about to turn. Discard your mourning survival work clothes and put on your ballgown, wash the dust of the past season's warfare off your feet and put on your dancing shoes . . . The stepsisters of hard toil, of intense, unrelenting warfare and survival mode have been given an edict of my courts of justice: No more!

My angelic host have been loosed to unfetter you from the enemy's grasp. It is time to dream again. I am about to let loose a tsunami of my goodness into your land of the living so that my Cinderellas' faith may be rebuilt, goodness upon goodness. Dream upon dream. No more isolation. No more pain. No more just surviving from day to day. No more bareness . . . exchange your worn out rags for my ball gown.

Beloved, take my hand in yours as I lead you to the carriage . . . for you are going to the ball!"

You are my most treasured possession. The apple of my eye. My beloved Cinderella,

Love,

Your Abba Father

YOUR GENTLENESS

SEER WORD: "YOUR GENTLENESS HAS MADE ME GREAT . . ."

*I*n the hardest times of your life, like David in Adullam and Ziglag, the Father does not despise your weak and sometimes faltering love for Him when all seems lost, but like He did with His beloved David, He esteems it as the true and genuine love that it is.

The enemy of your soul whispers, "You have failed God; your love for Him is weak. Your prayers won't be answered."

And so he condemns and accuses you. But, oh, beloved, if you feel you are faltering in your faith today, the Father said He has a word for you.

He said, "Look at the life of my son David. He was called with a mantle to be King over Israel and yet he ran and hid from Saul in the cave of Adullam, then was with Achish, a Philistine, in Ziglig."

This is now me (Wendy) speaking: The warfare was off the charts because, let me say it again, because of his powerful destiny ahead.

The Father continued, "I called David 'a man after my own heart.' He was greatly loved and adored by me and yet in the most pressing stressful times of his life he cried out to me in such anguish of soul. He experienced times of such desperation and despair, yet even in his weakest times I knew that his heart and the motivation of his heart were always after my heart. And so I called him 'greatly beloved. A man after my own heart."

Oh, dearest ones, in today's religious circles he would in all probability be ostracized by those who were walking in total victory and faith because, to them, David's faith was weak, he should never feel depressed or cry out in despair. But, David wrote this incredible thing about our Father:

YOUR RIGHT HAND HAS HELD ME UP, YOUR GENTLENESS HAS MADE ME GREAT.
(Psalm 18:35 KJV)

Your gentleness has made me great. God treated him with such gentleness throughout his entire life even though he made many mistakes and was so aware of his shortcomings.

He was called with a mantle to be King. He slew Goliath with great faith. What an exploit. But later he fled to the cave of Adullum to hide from Saul and it was there in Ziglag that he almost gave up. Imagine how he must have felt. The town destroyed, and houses were burned to the ground. Even his own team wanted to stone him. How far away his true destiny as King of Israel must have seemed when even his own team turned on him, wanting to kill him.

But, in it all David cried out to God. And God said, "Pursue and recover all . . ."

In the Ziglag years David wrote:

YOU NUMBER MY WANDERINGS; PUT MY TEARS INTO YOUR BOTTLE; ARE THEY NOT IN YOUR BOOK. WHEN I CRY OUT TO YOU, THEN MY ENEMIES WILL TURN BACK; THIS I KNOW, BECAUSE GOD IS FOR ME.
(Psalm 56:8–9 NKJV)

David knew that no matter how weak he felt or how great his despair, he could run to God and never be rejected in his weakness. God is gentle to us even in our Ziglag years. Oh, how He longs for us to know we are fully accepted even in our weakness.

HE HAS NOT DEALT WITH US ACCORDING TO OUR SINS, NOR PUNISHED US ACCORDING TO OUR INIQUITIES. FOR AS THE HEAVENS ARE HIGH ABOVE THE EARTH, SO GREAT IS HIS MERCY TOWARD THOSE WHO FEAR HIM. AS FAR AS THE EAST IS FROM THE WEST, SO FAR HAS HE REMOVED OUR TRANSGRESSIONS FROM US.

AS A FATHER PITIES HIS CHILDREN, SO THE LORD PITIES THOSE WHO FEAR HIM. FOR HE KNOWS OUR FRAME; HE REMEMBERS THAT WE ARE DUST.

(Psalm 103:10–14 KJV)

Oh, we serve such a compassionate Father. He knows our frame. He has such compassion on us. He is so kind. Beloved, we are walking through Adullam and Ziglag into our destiny. The fight has been fierce, at times ferocious, but we have not given up. And like David we will see destiny fulfilled and the Father's sovereign call upon our lives come to pass, for He loves us even in our weakest moments.

He is so, so beautiful. His gentleness will make us great.

THE AIRLIFT

SEER VISION: THE COURTS OF HEAVEN ARE FILLED WITH ACTIVITY, THE FATHER IS MOUNTING ONE OF THE GREATEST RESCUE MISSIONS HEAVEN HAS EVER SEEN.

Oh, beloved ones,

I had been asking Jesus and the Father so many questions to try and gain an understanding of the times and seasons that so, so many are experiencing. Multitudes of faithful champions of God have found themselves in a season almost pushed to the very limit of endurance. If you are one of the many who have been crying out to the Lord in desperation: 'Help, Father, rescue me, get me out of here,' the Father has said, "Enough is enough. I am mounting one of the greatest rescue missions Heaven has ever seen."

"And even as King David, my beloved servant, cried out to me 'Oh, God rescue me.' And as his cry reached my throne so the cries of my faithful called out ones have reached my throne."

Again, I feel I have to say, we have to be real. Being real and honest doesn't mean we don't have faith.

It doesn't mean that we don't believe in the finished work of the cross. Jesus was real with the Father. At Gethsemane when he was in such severe agony and intense trauma that he sweated blood, he cried out, *'Father, if it be your will let this cup pass from me but not my will but your will be done.'*

Last night when I was talking with Jesus I received a vision of modern day soldiers, the military – it seemed they were in Afghanistan. A group of soldiers had been cut off from their battalion because of the extreme warfare they had encountered. It seemed the enemy, in desperation, had launched one of the greatest strikes against their battalion using every ounce of firepower.

Many of the toughest soldiers were, seemingly, missing in action. A few had been able to send an SOS out to the base camp. But most communications were knocked out and replies were not getting through to them. They were hiding in caves. Isolated. Martialing all their courage and endurance not knowing if or when rescue was coming. Rations were almost gone. There was no help in sight.

What they didn't know but were desperately hoping for, was that unknown to them, base camp was launching an intensive airlift and rescue mission. Not one would be left behind. But they had hung on so long. Hiding. Scared. Isolated. They didn't know if and when they would be rescued.

The Father has launched the most powerful search and rescue mission on His faithful children's behalf. The most incredible shifts and miracles and a literal rescue from seemingly impossible circumstances that will literally fling us into destiny is taking place. Heaven is on the case. Heaven is on your case. Heaven is on your case. The airlift is beginning. The Holy Spirit knows exactly where you are – knows your coordinates and mighty angelic help is on the way.

Oh, beloved, I know so many of us have been through the most severe pressure but the command has gone out from our King, our mighty general. He will not fail us.

LAZARUS IS DEAD

SEER MESSAGE: THE FATHER'S HEART FOR ALL WHO HAVE BEEN UNDER IMMENSE PRESSURE, CRYING OUT TO HIM WITH THE QUESTION "WHY?" AND "LAZARUS IS DEAD. LORD, SOS, WHY ARE YOU LATE?"

Darling hearts,

I sense the Father had a message for you that was so, so important to Him. If we had been with Jesus when his dear friend Lazarus had died we would probably have cried, "Jesus. SOS. Emergency. Call 911, let's go now as fast as we can."

If it had been in this present day the scene would probably have gone like this: A flurry of all the disciples' iphones going off with texts and phone calls flying back and forth. Waking Jesus in the middle of the night having already booked his plane ticket, a car ready to rush him to the nearest airport. Bags packed. And imagine our response when he stayed where he was for three days!

Our hearts would have been confused and perplexed thinking – 'He's late, He's late. Doesn't he care? What are we going to tell Mary and Martha?'

And the Father said, "Tell my beloved children that I am not condemning then for crying out to me with the question 'Why?' when they feel pushed to their very limited in this season of transition. Crying, 'Daddy, Abba, why are you not moving, why are you late? Why are you late?' When like Lazarus it seems that all their promises aren't even just dying, it looks like they are dead. 'Can't you hear my SOS, Father? Why aren't you moving on my behalf? Even my beloved, only begotten Son cried out to me with the question: 'Why?'

And many of my children have been crying out to me with the question 'Why?' in this time of transition and they are feeling condemned.

And then He said, "My love is so great for you, beloved child. I am the Father of compassion, my understanding of you is inexhaustible. I knitted your parts together in your mother's womb. You were and still are my dream. Discern the enemy circumspectly in this season, beloved. He is the accuser of the brethren and the father of lies. The condemnation of your heart. In the Garden of Gethsemene, I watched my beloved, adored Son cry out in his agony and his anguish. His trauma affecting his soul to the extent that he sweated blood and on the cross, when he cried out in desperation and abandonment – 'Eloi, Eloi, Sabachtani . . . Father, Father, why have you forsaken me?' And I wept.

His *why* came from the depths of the desperate anguish in his soul of seeming abandonment and I looked on him and wept as I loved him and so too, today, beloved child, I look upon you and my heart is overwhelmed with compassion for you. For the enemy of your soul has sought to accuse your heart that your *why* was out of rebellion, but beloved child of my heart, your why was like my son's, out of the pain that in your earthly view you cannot fully comprehend. But, child of my heart, I tell you today that you see through a veil darkly for my rainbow of promise is now breaking through the clouds, for I am about to bring you out of the wilderness. Yes, you have cried out to me, 'Father, Father, how long, how long?' And I am stirred with compassion for you. I surely have never abandoned you and even as my Son's greatest anguish came before his resurrection, so, my child, it shall be with you. And even as Lazarus was in the tomb and it seemed that Jesus was late, too late, death came before resurrection. I tell you the resurrection of your dreams is in the seeming silence of the glaring delay – I am moving people and circumstances behind the scenes. Oh, trust me, my child. Trust me that even as Jesus said to Lazarus, 'Come forth,' after it seemed that every hope had gone, trust me that I am about to move in acceleration upon your life and say: 'Lazarus come forth, promises come forth, dreams and visions that seem to have died, now come forth. Hearts' desires that have seemingly been delayed and deferred, now come forth. I have not forsaken you. I have not forgotten you. I am about to come to your town to stand outside your tomb and cry, 'Lazarus come forth.' Your resurrection, your restitution, your restoration is finally here. Trust Me. Trust Me. Trust me, beloved child, I will not be late."

Love, your Abba Father.

STRETCHED TO THE LIMIT

SEER DISCERNMENT FOR ALL WHOSE MINDS, FAITH, EMOTION AND WILL ARE SO STRETCHED TO THE LIMIT.

*D*aniel, Joseph, King David, our Lord Jesus all had to walk where you are walking now in your journey. Excruciating as it is, the enemy's intention was to wear out their souls so they would quit before they were released into their world changing mandates. We cannot quit now. Yes, it is excruciating.

For me, after four years of literally walking through what at times has seemed like sheer hell and the valley of the shadow, like so many of you in this season of transition, I rise each morning sometimes clinging on by a thread.

The place where the rubber hits the road.
I had a great sensing that many of us are in a dispensation – a season of the Double Edged Sword. In this season is something that believers, so often in our theology, shy away from and that is the mystery. What we see through a veil darkly is the workings of ENDURANCE and PERSEVERANCE and PATIENCE and TENACITY that the Father in His all-knowing omniscience has been combining in our tapestries in this present, soon to be past, season. We can run ... I've run. We can hide .... I tried to hide. We can put our heads under the blankets and try to sleep it off into oblivion and escape. But we cannot escape the knowledge that before

each incredible, world shaking breakthrough of mandates that would literally change nations and the world Daniel was in the Lion's den. Jospeh was in the pit and then in prison. David was in the cave at Adullam. Jesus was in Gethsemene. They were where so many of us feel we are today. Trapped, betrayed and abandoned by those closest to them, pushed to the very limit.

Jesus was so anguished he literally sweated blood but after, when the season of intense warfare and suffering was over ... Daniel was given the mysteries of heaven and prophetic revelation to the end times. Joseph became the deliverer of the entire nation of Egypt. David moved out of Adullam up to Jerusalem and became King of Israel and Jesus became the whole of mankind's deliverer and Savior!

The enemy put each of these champions of God under the most excruciating, intensive duress with only one goal – that they would become so weary, so hopeless and despairing, so shaken in their faith that they would faint and give up before they fulfilled their mandates that would change their nations and the world. The enemy's intention was to wear their souls down with such intense warfare that these champions would quit. I know so many of us are feeling pressures so intense that we, even as seasoned warriors, have never experienced before in our long walk with Jesus.

But we are the Daniels and Josephs and Davids and our oh, so incredible beloved, beautiful Jesus, our high Priest and intercessor is so, so close to us, urging us, praying for us in this season having been moved by great compassion to walk us through the last intensity of the battle before we break through.

We will break through. You will break through and your testimony will change your world and many of you will literally change the WORLD.

Father, I pray for all of us,

Grant us the courage, the endurance not to quit.

Oh, compassionate Father, release your tokens of goodness to our hearts in the land of the living. Imbue us with fresh grace. Fresh courage. Fresh hope, as we walk the final steps out of the seeming wilderness into our breakthroughs, our mandates, our callings.

MY FIRST YEAR –
A LITTLE BIT OF MY STORY

*D*arling heart, if you have just stepped into the tsunami of divorce and are lying sobbing in your bed, your hair not brushed, let alone washed, unable to cook or eat or even to function and not wanting to wake up tomorrow, on meds and whatever else, doing anything to try to alleviate your pain, we, too, a whole band of wounded warriors, love you and have been there as well.

We truly, truly, understand your indescribable pain.

There are so, so many who have made it through and are walking on the other side.

In the sunshine.

Following their new rainbow.

Some of us, myself included, are still in transition on the battlefield, but a long way from where we were able to start living again, bit by bit.

I woke up in a surreal nightmare, not wanting to live.

I had not only lost my husband and best friend of 30 years, but I had a double hit in that I had also lost my co-visionary and ministry partner.

Nothing eased the pain. I moved into the small home in the German colony of Jerusalem that we had both picked out.

And I, the supreme creative homemaker, didn't even have the strength to unpack or arrange my furniture. My beloved friend Liz arranged my home.

My incredible friends, who will confess they had wanted to live with ice packs on their heads for the past three years, Marilyn, Liz, Lois, Shirley and Cecile, literally kept me alive.

With their love, their prayers, their unrelenting care for me.

They did relays on me, traveling to Israel to be with me.

The truth was that nothing, no beloved friends, absolutely nothing, could take away the pain.

As Israel was so far away, and our former family home was in the divorce mix, I was left sometimes for weeks on my own.

Lying in my bed, with my faithful cat, in pajamas, hardly able to eat, sobbing for hours.

I sobbed in bed and on the floor, but mostly I sobbed flung down headlong on the grass in the tiny Jerusalem garden.

All I could utter was, "I have no life . . . I have no life . . ."

I couldn't read for the first year. Not even a magazine. Couldn't bear to look in a shop.

I couldn't watch television. Pinterest and Etsy and Ebay, all of which I loved, held nothing for me anymore.

It seemed as though something indefinable in my very inner core had been broken.

And even though I loved the Father, I had no idea how to fix it.

No matter how much prayer – and I received loads.

No matter how much I cried out to God.

I was a sobbing, needy, broken mess with not an ounce of will to live.

What made it harder, I believe, is that the divorce came at the exact same time as my children left home.

So instead of the normal four . . . there was one . . . me!

I had always been so independent.

I had loved my alone time.

But now the tables had turned.

"But you loved God, Wendy," you may say.

"How could you be so broken?"

The answer is that I discovered that for so very many of us, pain often doesn't, in fact, drive us to God.

It left me hit by a tsunami, like a bewildered, desperate five-year-old clutching at straws.

I would lie for hours at a time crying, sometimes screaming,

'Father, no more pain ... please ... please ... no more pain!'

It was as though the heavens were brass.

Oh, but yes, my beloved, incredible heavenly Father was there.

He was always there.

But I just couldn't connect.

Couldn't make the connection.

But He was so good to me.

He sent me my friends.

He sent me the kindest of people.

From the Israeli taxi driver who left a rose on my doorstep, to the doctor who would walk me down the street several evenings a week. To my wonderful Israeli hairdresser who had been divorced.

To Benny Hinn who would take me out for dinner each time he was in Israel and check on me.

And to my beloved friend Kim Clement who took me and the kids to dinner whenever he was in Jerusalem and said, "Wendy, I'm your covering now ..."

But none of it.

None of it healed my heart.

How I managed to go on TV at that stage ... only Heaven knows.

The first part of my real healing came when Kat Kerr came on my program and prayed for me, releasing soul ties.

She literally prayed Rory out of my soul.

And from that day to this, I was freed from any and all grief concerning him.

The major, major attack for me, on my heart, was not the loss of Rory. No, it was the agonizing, utterly unbearable loneliness of being alone after twenty-seven years of male companionship.

No one to share with.

No one to dream with.

No one to put the rubbish out.

No one to kiss or hold at night.

It eroded me, gnawing at my inner core,

And nothing eased the pain.

My girlfriends didn't ease that space.

I had been so used to masculine energy for over thirty years.

I remember sobbing my eyes out like a crazy woman standing behind a couple at check-in at Heathrow Terminal Five, because I wasn't a couple anymore.

I was terrified to maneuver my way through the seemingly sprawling metropolis.

I remember trying desperately to get my luggage off the baggage claim and breaking down in tears because I couldn't lift my bag off the conveyor belt. Oh, my . . .

These are some of the things we miss.

A big strong man to help us with all the things our husbands did for us.

But very slowly I grew.

Today I can traverse Terminal 5 at Heathrow almost blindfolded.

I have flown multitudes of times to Tel Aviv, Oslo, Sydney, Melbourne, Dubai, Cyprus, Cape Town, Orlando, Los Angeles, Nashville, Dallas, San Francisco even to Las Vegas and on and on!

I don't even notice when couples are in front of me.

From not being able to bear spending a day alone, I can quite happily spend multiple days writing and working and, although it's still not my best (I so love people), I'm okay with it.

I'm back to reading and writing and have just started being creative at home again.

I love having the teenagers and their friends, sleeping in my bed, on my day bed and on my sofa!

I have been for huge amounts of prayer and deliverance and I have the most incredible Christian therapist, who is now my beautiful friend, who has walked me through a lot of buried trauma.

I can now laugh with my married girlfriends.

I decided not to date – well apart from one fling which I didn't realize would be just a fling.

Oh, please, never, never, do what I did.

Our hearts are not strong enough.

We are each a prize of untold value to be treasured and adored and loved.

Nothing less.

You deserve a husband or wife who will treasure your heart.

Who can see you at your very worst, even in your raw pain and still see beyond your actions, to the incredible treasure and beauty that your heart holds.

You are worth the ring.

You are worth commitment.

You are worth covenant.

I wasn't able to write for almost three years, and here I am, having completed book five of the Chronicles of Brothers series.

For the first time on a Friday night, if I'm alone, I can walk into a restaurant in London and very happily absorb the atmosphere.

Breakthrough has finally started to happen.

I fought a ferocious battle for my book, TV and merchandising rights to come back for more than three years after the divorce.

Finally, all my intellectual property came back into my hands, just as the Father had promised.

And following straight on that a second miracle – I signed the Chronicles of Brothers books with one of the largest publishers in the world – HarperCollins.

As I write this, I've just returned from an amazing evening event with top authors in London, have just completed book five, *End of Days*, and now travel to speak at Bethel in Redding, California. And we are about to enter development of the Chronicles TV series.

And so, beloved, beautiful friends, the journey of restoration continues. Watch this space. And I'll watch yours!

Join our incredible family on Facebook, oh, they're so amazing – you'll be literally washed with love.

Here for you,

From my heart,

Wendy x

EPILOGUE
WOUNDED WARRIORS

We are living in a transitional season as a body of believers. Today, we're through the past several decades the Holy Spirit has faithfully been highlighting and drawing our attention decade by decade to the priorities of Heaven with different weights of focus on certain scriptural truths.

These truths have been highlighted to be embedded in our hearts and minds for that particular season.

For example in the 70s and 80s, the Holy Spirit began to illuminate our hearts and our spirits to the importance of the Word of Faith; raising up apostolic teachers whose sole focus for their lives was to teach us faith, our confession and victory emphasizing the fact that we are seated in Jesus Christ in Heavenly places.

The challenge to many of us as believers, is that instead of moving onward in the same season as the Holy Spirit moves to highlight another truth, because we tend to embrace what we become comfortable with, we have at times stayed in a past season of the Holy Spirit for years instead of being like the Sons of Issachar who rightly divided the word of truth and discerned the timings and the seasons of the Father Himself.

For instance, many, many of us stayed completely focused on the 'Word' when the Holy Spirit was moving the Church into the next season of Heaven to Earth, which was now to place as much weight on the Spirit as He had placed on the Word, thus becoming a move with the weight of Heaven's glory resting on both the Word AND the Spirit.

Even today, nearly 45 years later, there are those who have still never moved into the full timeline of Heaven, not realizing that each major truth in different dispensations is supposed to be grafted into our souls and spirit as an eternal deposit, but that it is a portion of the 360 degrees – not the whole.

The Holy Spirit is continually speaking and revealing himself with new facets of himself, our Lord Jesus and the Father.

This has opened the door to a religious spirit, which the enemy has at times used against believers.

I believe with all my heart that, in this season, the Holy Spirit's mandate is to reveal 1 Corinthians 13 and to deliver many of us from a religious spirit, that this present and next dispensation is vitally connected to LOVE.

Where there is true fervent love between each of us, there is no fear in being known as we truly are for we know we are not only truly loved by God but by our brothers and sisters in Christ.

Where there is love there is no veil of shame because we see each other through the eyes of love.

Where there is love, there is a laying down of our lives for each other, which causes divine, eternally forged friendships and relationships which are marked by their authenticity, transparency and loyalty.

Love is the trademark of our King of kings.

To be truly loved and embraced delivers us from our humanity and secret challenges, because when we are truly loved by our brothers and sisters in Christ, we have the courage to confess our sins and humanity in transparency to each other and the result is that we may be healed.

I believe that the Father is unrelentingly breaking down our walls of shame, of fear, of reputation, of religious seeds that have infiltrated our heart, to prepare us for the greatest outpouring that the secular world will ever see.

For they will know we are Christians by our love one for another.

What are you saying, Wendy?

Beloved heart – We still find ourselves in a transitional season as wounded warriors – we are terrified to be vulnerable because of being misunderstood, betrayed, looked upon as a failure.

Never before have there been so many champions crying every night from bereavements, broken hearts, brutal divorces, devastating losses of loved ones, of businesses, of visions and ministries.

In the military, the wounded in frontline combat receive the most violent attack and when they arrive back from Afghanistan or Iraq wounded they are treated with honor and with such appreciation by their leaders and compatriots and even more so by their families on the home front – their physical wounds are attended to as the highest priority.

But the post-traumatic stress that many have endured from the trauma of the battles they have faced are also attended to.

In the USA those who have been wounded in combat receive the Purple Heart.

The military learned from Vietnam. Brave and valiant men arrived back to shame – there were no accolades for a war that was unfinished and never fully won.

Decades later, many Vietnam veterans are still the broken, the homeless – never having received the true recognition for the incredible sacrifice they made.

Thousands upon thousands never recovered from the post-traumatic stress from all they had witnessed and experienced of the literal depths of the hell that they lived through.

So they became addicts, alcoholics, junkies, their subconscious desperately trying to escape the trauma still lodged so deeply in their souls. These men, who sacrificed their lives every day, who lived through the most savage of battles, should have been our heros but instead a great veil of shame was cast across so many, many, brave men.

What do we as the Church do with our wounded?

This will not be popular, but beloved, so often as the Church, we treat our wounded like the soldiers that returned home from Vietnam.

Not looking beneath the surface to realize that many of our wounded today are those who are God's finest and His champions. Those who have faced the full assault of the enemy upon their lives.

Those who did not stay on the home front, but instead set out to do great and mighty exploits for their King.

We are in a WAR.

We can dismiss this fact; ignore it; pretend it doesn't exist but it doesn't change the fact – WE ARE IN A WAR.

Yes, we understand that Jesus Christ had the victory.

Yes, we understand that we are seated in Heavenly places with Christ.

What I am going to say next may be controversial but it is TOTALLY scriptural.

Peter was hung upside down.

James was beheaded.

This was the Apostles' fate AFTER THE RESURRECTION OF JESUS CHRIST.

In our nice, safe, comfortable little Christian world where we believe for our houses and cars, we try to preserve our safe, well preserved world with everything we have and we call it faith. And yes, it is faith but it is also THE HOMEFRONT.

But, oh, how some of us condemn the wounded warriors who have been so targeted and assailed by the enemy because of the call and mandate and unrelenting fervor to fulfil His call ON THE BATTLEFRONT.

And so the wounded warrior has often been swept under the proverbial church carpet.

If Paul were here today and was crucified, and James was beheaded, many of us may have whispered like the sanctimonious Pharisees and Sadducees, "Where was their FAITH? They didn't have enough faith.

They failed, they obviously didn't confess the Word enough or they would never have been hurt."

It was the Apostle Paul who wrote so strongly in his letters to the Church.

> . . . BUT "HE WHO GLORIES, LET HIM GLORY IN THE LORD."
> FOR NOT HE WHO COMMENDS HIMSELF IS APPROVED, BUT WHOM
> THE LORD COMMENDS . . .
> (2 Corinthians 1:17–18 KJV)

But in this present age, we look at those who are facing the furnace like Daniel or the pit and prison like Joseph and whisper among ourselves, 'They must have sin in their life. They don't have MY measure of faith.'

What might we have said to our Lord Jesus in Gethsemane?

"Lord Jesus,

Why are you sweating blood?

You've taught us for so long about faith in your Heavenly Father.

You slept through the storm.

How can you be experiencing this on your great commission?

Trembling in the garden in such extreme trauma that you're sweating blood?"

Oh, darling hearts, we deny that we are but we all are so religious at times.

And when finally Jesus cried out on the cross: *'Eloi, Eloi, Sabachtani,'* maybe many of us may have been embarrassed and been among those disheartened that their Savior could cry out that he had been forsaken and maybe we would have disowned Jesus in our bewilderment and fled.

'Jesus, you're our fearless leader. What are you doing crying up there?'

Endurance. Perseverance.

Before I was divorced, I am so ashamed to confess, that the agony of the single, deserted mother or those divorced hardly touched me. I was so complacent, married for 27 years that their heartbreak never entered my comfortable, married world.

I had no conception of how divorce literally tore one's soul and family apart, how so many people were going to bed soaking their pillows in tears, dreading to wake up to a new day.

How many had lost their homes, their savings, their pets, living like nomads with no clue how they would support themselves in their later years.

My Facebook is literally a testament to these brave, valiant, courageous souls who have clung to the Lord with every fiber of their being – traumatized yet still believing.

Abandoned and deserted but still holding fast to the Father.

They are today's heroes.

And yet, the Church is not always a safe place for them.

Jesus always ministered to each situation individually because only he knew the motivation and intent of the heart of a person.

The reason why?

Desperate pain and trauma can drive us to things that in our previous tidy, sheltered worlds, we would never have dreamt we would do.

And yet, how the Lord has compassion on these ones and is so deeply moved that in the hardest and darkest and loneliest of times a cry reaches him from these one that still says, ' I love you, Abba.'

Oh, he looks down from Heaven and sees such courage. Such valor. Such fortitude.

And yet many, so many, are still ostracized by the Church.

THE ULTIMATE TEST – Where is the goodness of God?

On our journey coming out of intense trauma, loss, bereavement and seeming abandonment, each of us is faced with the ultimate testing of our faith.

By the testing of our faith, I'm not talking about faith to believe for cars and houses and lands or material things, I'm talking about the valley of the shadow when our very history with God is put on the line.

And I've found that in my own walk with God, when it comes down to the wire, the ultimate test in the very secret and hidden depths of our heart is: 'Father, I have served you with all my heart. Forgive me, please, all my besetting weaknesses and humanities.' And then the question arises, the one that we hide so skillfully away from even our most trusted loved ones – and from ourselves.

How, when I have tried with all my heart unreservedly to worship and serve the Father and our Lord Jesus, how could this happen to me?

And then the terrible gnawing, unutterable ache of – where is the goodness of God?

IN ALL THIS YOU GREATLY REJOICE, THOUGH NOW FOR A LITTLE WHILE
YOU MAY HAVE HAD TO SUFFER GRIEF IN ALL KINDS OF TRIALS. THESE
HAVE COME SO THAT THE PROVEN GENUINENESS OF YOUR FAITH —
OF GREATER WORTH THAN GOLD, WHICH PERISHES EVEN THOUGH
REFINED BY FIRE — MAY RESULT IN PRAISE, GLORY AND HONOR WHEN
JESUS CHRIST IS REVEALED. THOUGH YOU HAVE NOT SEEN HIM,
YOU LOVE HIM; AND EVEN THOUGH YOU DO NOT SEE HIM NOW, YOU
BELIEVE IN HIM AND ARE FILLED WITH AN INEXPRESSIBLE AND
GLORIOUS JOY.
(1 Peter 1:6–8 KJV)

So that the proven genuineness of our faith, that does not mean faith in our faith but our faith in the Father and His only begotten, beloved Son, Jesus Christ which is counted in Heaven as more precious than gold may stay steady when all hell breaks loose around us.

And it is at exactly at the most immensely pressurized time of our lives, at the point of the furnace and the wilderness and the seeming unending desert, when the enemy of our souls strikes the hardest with utter ruthlessness and cruelty and whispers to our heart . . .

'How can God be good?'

For months we can be resilient, but when the months become years, the temptation to utter despair through seeming hope deferred, that is the exact moment that the age old question from the father of lies himself gnaws at our souls.

And silently, so silently we ask ourselves with agony in our hearts, 'Father, where is your goodness in the land of the living . . . ?

Are you really good?'

That is when true courage is tested.

That is when the rubber hits the road.

That is when our faith is tested like molten gold being purified.

To hold steady in our season of greatest loss, despair and trauma and not to succumb to the devil's lies about the character of our ever benevolent King of Glory.

Lucifer lost his intimacy and firsthand knowledge and experience of the overwhelming goodness of God when he and a third of the angelic host committed insurrection and rebelled against our Heavenly Father.

And today, banished from all intimacy, cut off from all communion with our Father, eternally disconnected from His wondrous glory and presence, and from his GOODNESS – our enemy – the accuser of our souls -has one overriding intensely evil strategy.

And that is to take our souls captive by defacing our Father's character and accusing the Father to us.

'How when you have served God faithfully could He have taken your son, your daughter, your wife, your husband, your business, your ministry away from you?

'How could He have allowed you to go through such devastation, such intense trauma and loss?

'How could He have allowed your dream and destiny that once was so vibrant and glowing with such promise to seemingly fall to the ground and die?'

And then his finale -

'Your God has forsaken you.

He has abandoned you.

Where is His goodness?'

But, beloved, hold steady.

Oh, beloved heart, cling to your Abba Father with all your might, even if you have found yourself silently running from Him in your despair and bewilderment – hold steady.

For, our oh, so beautiful Lord Jesus is walking towards you, his nail scarred hands outstretched to you, looking at only you – with such tender mercies, such infinite compassion saying:

"Oh, beloved storm tossed, hurting child,

"I have been tempted in every form that you are suffering now.

"When I was in Gethsemane I experienced such intense mental trauma and agony, that I sweated blood.

"My child, I have experienced the worst of betrayals.

"I have experienced rejection by my own.

"I have experienced mental anguish that bought me to my knees.

"Oh, my child, it was when I was finally at breaking point on the cross, at the point of the seeming abandonment by the greatest love of my life, my beloved adored Father, my ABBA, that I too cried, '*Eloi Eloi Sabachtani?*' My God, my God, why have you forsaken me? The intensity of the trauma, of seeming abandonment that my soul could barely endure.

"I have taken your pain.

"I have taken your anguish.

"I have borne your abandonment.

"And yet you say, 'But Jesus, I know you took it but I am going through it.'

"Oh, child, beloved, child of my heart,

"Know this, that the enemy of your soul, when he has looked upon you has seen my mark . . . my calling . . . my mantle upon you, and an imprint of my Father's destiny for you.

"And in his rage and ferocity, he has attacked and assigned demonic forces to drive you to your knees.

"That is the fellowship of my sufferings.

"BECAUSE you bear my image.

"BECAUSE you are marked in destiny by my Father.

"BECAUSE you are our champion and our called out one, you have been marked by Heaven.

"And assigned by the forces of hell.

"I am your great High Priest.

"Your intercessor.

"Your deliverer.

"Your redeemer.

"Your rescuer.

"Your restorer.

"Hold steady, my child.

"Hold steady, yes, even as the tears flow, hold steady.

"I said I would never forsake you and that I am with you always.

"All my Father's promises are yes and Amen, for the Father Himself weeps for you in your anguish.

"But, like He knew when I cried out in anguish to Him on the cross,

"Oh, beloved faithful child,

"Your Father preordained you to be His called out one.

"His champion.

"And even as He weeps for you,

"Lean into Him.

"Quiet your soul.

"For as He weeps, He would whisper to your broken, traumatized heart,

'Hold steady my valiant son, my valiant daughter,

You are almost through.'

"And He turns to the enemy of your soul with an all-consuming fire in His eyes.

"'No further!' is His command.

"For truly you have stayed the course.

"You have heard of the endurance of Job and you have seen the Lord's purpose and how He richly blessed him in the end in as much as the Lord is:

'FULL OF PITY AND COMPASSION AND TENDERNESS AND MERCY . . .'
(James 5:11, KJV)"

FINAL THOUGHTS AND PRAYERS

Beloved friend,

I know that so many of you have been through such hard times in this past season of transition.

Times of abandonment.

Times of deep grieving and sorrow.

Times when deferred hope has made your heart sick.

And the cry that has rung up to the Father's altar from the very core of your being has been, "Father, NO more pain!

"I feel like I am clinging on by a thread."

But today, your beloved Father, the Father of all mercy and pity, who knows and infinitely understands that your frame is dust and yet you are His great treasure, says:

"Come walk with me, beloved child."

He whispers,

"Come, walk with me in my garden.

"Come, lay your head on my chest,

"And clutch my robe and, as we share the secret things together,

"I will stroke your head.

"Know this, beloved child of my heart, the tsunami is over, the robbery and grief and loss of yesterday are swiftly coming to an end."

And our great and marvelous Emperor would lift your face tenderly to His and whisper,

"It is time to rise. Come away, my beloved, come away and dance with me."

And, as He gently raises you to your feet and places a wreath of flowers upon your head, in a moment the flowers are turning into a golden crown and, as He looks upon you, oh, weary one, He smiles.

He is so, so, proud of you, beloved one, for the crown is none other than the victor's crown, the overcomer's crown.

"But, Daddy, I have been so weak," you whisper.

"I have clung on with all my might,

"But I have stumbled and fallen,

"I have cried so many tears."

And the Father would take you so tenderly into His arms, as tears falling from His eyes bring healing to your shattered heart. He whispers,

"Even in your very weakest moment, when you felt as though you were falling, yet still you loved me.

"Still you were faithful to me.

"Still you cried out to me. That was courage indeed.

"And so, beloved, your reward is now about to be released by my angelic messengers from Heaven itself."

And as He smiles into your eyes so gloriously,

He twirls you around and cries, rejoicing,

"My beloved son, beloved daughter,

IT IS TIME FOR THE DANCE!"

Your incredible, majestic, compassionate, the most beautiful of ALL, your heavenly Father.

xxx

There was once one who used to dance uproariously with the Father,

Until his heart was lifted up through pride.

He was banished from the Father's dance and from His presence for all eternity.

And he was defeated through the cross by Jesus' sacrifice at Calvary.

His jealousy and hatred for each of us who now walk and talk and dance with the Father knows no bounds. Oh, beloved, no matter how shattered your dreams may be, no matter how broken and abandoned your heart, lift up your weary hands and put on your dancing shoes.

For it is He who contends with you . . . for the Father's dance. Oh, greatly beloved, your Father is wooing you . . . entreating you . . .

Oh, so earnestly . . . oh, so tenderly . . . back into His dance.

CONTACT DETAILS

For news, updates, including live chat with Wendy and lots more, join our incredible Facebook family.

https://www.facebook.com/wendyalec777
https://twitter.com/Wendy_Alec
https://www.instagram.com/wendyalec

Other Books by Wendy Alec

Visions from Heaven –
Visitations to My Father's Chamber

ISBN 978–0–9928063–0–9

Wendy Alec recounts a series of extraordinary, supernatural encounters with the Father, following a season of deep, personal trauma.

If Heaven itself has seemed so silent ... so, so very silent at your time of deepest need ... the Father's answers to these questions will bring surprise, challenge, immense encouragement and such hope.

Journal of the Unknown Prophet

ISBN 978–0955237713

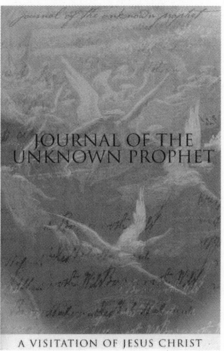

A VISITATION OF JESUS CHRIST

Wendy Alec's powerful book is a divine revelation of the Lord Jesus
Christ and His cry for a deeper intimacy with each and
every person on earth.

For the unbeliever, it represents a profound picture of who Jesus
really is and how much He cares – how He has always been there
for them, and how He wants to enrich their lives.
For the believer, it is an extraordinary challenge to walk in the
fullness of everything God has in store for His beloved children.

Available now from your local book store
or from Amazon and other on-line retailers.

The Chronicles of Brothers Series

www.chroniclesofbrothers.com

For more information on the Chronicles of Brothers
including other books in the series, the characters,
live chat with the author, author's blog and lots more.

The Fall of Lucifer

ISBN 978–0310090977

Messiah: The First Judgement

ISBN 978–0310090984

Son of Perdition

ISBN 978–0310090991

A Pale Horse

ISBN 978–0310091004

End of Days

ISBN 978–0310091011

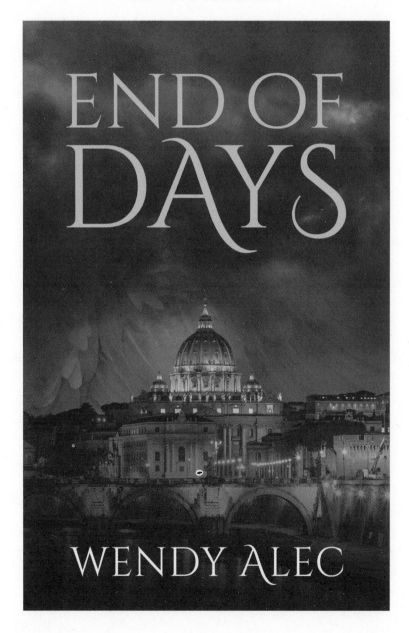

Wendy Alec, the author, was born in London, England.
Coming from a background in the arts and media,
she was the Programming and Creative Director of GOD TV,
a leading global religious network that she co-founded.
Prophet, seer, writer and broadcaster, Wendy travels extensively
speaking and teaching and is also the author of the
epic best-selling 'Chronicles of Brothers' series of novels.
Wendy has two grown children and makes her home in the UK.